D0389660

EPICTETUS
SENECA
ZENO
MARCUS AURELIUS

WISE UP

Also by Karen Duffy

Model Patient

Backbone

WISE UP

IRREVERENT ENLIGHTENMENT from
a **MOTHER** Who's Been Through It

KAREN DUFFY

SEAL PRESS
New York

Cover design by Ann Kirchner
Cover photography © Ondrea Barbe
Cover copyright © 2022 Hachette Book Group, Inc.

Seal Press
Hachette Book Group
1290 Avenue of the Americas, New York, NY 10104
www.sealpress.com
@sealpress

Printed in the United States of America
First Edition: April 2022

Published by Seal Press, an imprint of Perseus Books, LLC, a subsidiary of Hachette Book Group, Inc. The Seal Press name and logo is a trademark of the Hachette Book Group.

Illustrations by John Eder

Print book interior design by Linda Mark

Library of Congress Cataloging-in-Publication Data
Names: Duffy, Karen, 1961– author.
Title: Wise up : irreverent enlightenment from a mother who's been through it / Karen Duffy.
Description: First edition. | New York : Seal Press, 2022. | Includes bibliographical references.
Identifiers: LCCN 2021047712 | ISBN 9781541620476 (hardcover) | ISBN 9781541620483 (epub)
Subjects: LCSH: Duffy, Karen, 1961- | Duffy, Karen, 1961—Family. | Motherhood—United States—Miscellanea. | Mothers and sons—United States—Miscellanea. | Mothers—United States—Biography. | Wisdom—Miscellanea. | Conduct of life—Miscellanea.
Classification: LCC HQ759 .D825 2022 | DDC 306.874/3092—dc23/eng/20211217
LC record available at https://lccn.loc.gov/2021047712

ISBNs: 9781541620476 (hardcover), 9781541620483 (ebook)

LSC-C

Printing 1, 2022

For John Fortune Lambros and Jack Augustine Lambros

There is not a particle of my love that is not yours.

—James Joyce

Contents

CONTENTS

INTRODUCTION

Dear Reader,

When you're in a bookstore browsing titles, it's not easy to decide which book to blow your hard-earned cash on. Some people just read the summary on the jacket flap or look at the back cover to see who praised it. I assure you that if you take just a moment to read on, I will persuade you that this tome is worth every penny of your investment. If the salesclerk is burning a hole in the back of your head with his glare, slide over behind a bookcase and keep reading.

You come from a long line of survivors. You are the latest link in an unbroken chain of ancestors. The Latin root for "survive" is "supervivere," meaning to live beyond, live longer, and continue in existence after the death of another. You are the descendant of people who lived through natural and man-made disasters, wars, pandemics, and cataclysms of all kinds. They endured pain, grief, fear, and loss. They outlasted quarantines. This is your genetic inheritance.

You are humanity's greatest upgrade. You are a miracle, a wonder. You are forty trillion cells thrumming with life force.

There is an original, radiant, and unrepeatable brilliance within you. This is the raw material from which we shape our lives.

Now that we agree that you are alive, we can also agree that you have many big questions. Why were you born? How can you be a good person? How many cannibals would your body feed? And of course, how shall you live? Will the course of your life be determined by drift or by decision? Don't we owe it to our intrepid ancestors to do our best to live a good life of meaning and purpose?

Imagine you could watch a film of your life, from birth to death. What would it take for you to jump out of your chair, start pumping your fists in the air, and shout, "Yes, this is it! This is a good life! This is a life well lived!"?

How *do* you live a good life? By defining a philosophy for living. A philosophy is nothing more than some simple rules for yourself. If you have a grasp on how the world works and have a sense of how to behave toward others, you have a philosophy of life. It is a framework, a backbone, a set of principles or guidelines that give your life direction and prevent drift.

It is never too late to get smarter or be better. Whether you just came out of a coma, emerged from self-isolation, or are just out poking around the bookstore, you are blessed with life and you are one of the luckiest people to have ever drawn a breath. It is up to you to make the most of your time here. We say, "you only live once," but truthfully, you live every day—you only die once.

Every day is an opportunity to examine your life, to be inspired, to take small actions, and make improvements and corrections that will steer you toward the goal of being a good person. My life has been greatly enhanced by applying the principles of Stoic wisdom. The simplicity of the philosopher Epictetus's quote,

"If you make beautiful choices, so too, will you be," reverberated through me like a firecracker in a cymbal factory.

I have distilled the practical wisdom of the Stoics into a book of breezy letters to my son. I do some of my best communicating in letters, and I hope to set off an explosion in you, too. If your ultimate goal is to stand up and cheer for your life, the journey begins with a philosophy.

Life doesn't give you a manual. But it does give you a mother.

Thank you for reading this far.

Sincerely,
The Author

P.S. The margin is an ancient device found even in very early written scrolls. Its original purpose was not legibility or doodling; that came later. The margin was used because of the appetites of the rodents that would gnaw and eat the edges of paper. This is rat food!

1

WHY I WRITE YOU LETTERS

Dear Jack,

I am writing to you from a body that once carried the promise of yours. Now, when I embrace you, it feels like I am hugging a bicycle: all muscle and bone, sinew and angles. The sharp blades of your shoulders, the stony protuberances of your elbows, the xylophone of ribs, and the knots of spine are far from the soft squish of the ten-pound newborn who cannonballed out of the business end of the birth canal.

You are my only son, and your life has been a rush of moments, from meeting you as you inhaled for the first time as an air-breathing mammal, to applauding as you took your first steps as a toddler, then racing behind you as you scooted to preschool, and cheering as you skated toward the Pee Wee hockey team where you found your people and your place in the world. Now you're expanding from boy to adolescent, to late teen, to early adult. I carried you in my arms and one day you outgrew this and I set you down and never, ever picked you up again.*

* I looked up the saddest things in the world and this was at the top of the list.

The one consolidative experience shared by the entirety of human life is the months-long gestation, folded up like a tiny lawn chair, inside a woman's body. You existed in me, and at your birth you began your life and I began a new life as well, one in which your well-being is always within the dominion of my consciousness. To parent is to become inextricably snared in the conflict of cheering on your independence and worrying about your self-sovereignty.

Puberty is an origin story. The ability to transform from child to full-grown human is a superpower. Your body is shape-shifting, and every sense is affected. Your taste in food, the music you listen to, and what you read have all evolved. Your ravenous appetite is fueling your growth. You are stronger and hairier, and a human crop sprayer of B.O. You see your peers and your romantic partners through a new lens. You now possess the terrifying power to contribute to the creation of another human being with the cells of your body. Yes, your body is a temple, but after crew practice it is less a house of worship and more like a Coachella festival for bacteria.

I witnessed your growth and transition from baby, to boy, to man. The stages of development progressed with breathless agility. I miss the big, bald, melon-headed Jack the Lad with the gap-tooth smile. Well, you do play hockey, so maybe I'll see that toothless grin again. How many more times will I remember that when you wanted to be freed from your crib, you would call me "Sweetheart," "Darling," or "Beauty," the names you heard your father call me when he wanted my attention? How many more times will I tell the story about your kindergarten class calendar, when you drew a naked picture of me in the bathtub reading a book? It was mostly a stick figure, but you went anatomically and hirsutely accurate and drew a lady bush that looked like a raccoon was sitting on my lap, taking a bath with me. That calendar page, which was displayed during the longest month of October, earned me the nickname "Crockett" from the wiseass moms at your elementary school. How many more times will I answer to that sobriquet? On reflection, I do hope that part of my life is ended.

As one of my favorite writers, Paul Bowles, wrote in *The Sheltering Sky*, "How many more times will you remember a certain afternoon of your childhood, some afternoon that's so deeply a part of your being that you cannot even conceive of your life without it? Perhaps four or five times more. Perhaps not even that. How many times will you watch the full moon rise? Perhaps twenty, yet it all seems limitless."

There is a built-in obsolescence to the parent-child relationship. Your childhood seemed boundless, but now you are on the precipice of adulthood. To see the gentleman you have grown into is the greatest happiness of my life. I recognize that I am no longer the sun you once revolved around. You have spun off to create your own new life in a new orbit. My job was to raise an independent progeny. Your job is to be independent. We each have done our jobs. Well done, both of us.

When you were younger, I attempted to explain the physiobiology of your maturation. One of the chemicals swimming in your cojones is the hormone testosterone. This powerful secretion kicks in to customize your face with zits and whiskers and grow muscles and hair. It synthesizes the sinister vapors emanating from your gym bag, delivering a roundhouse kick of adolescent man-stink to the olfactory sense. It fuels your ascent from boy to man. This chemical's job is the evolutionary command that directs you to pass on your genetic material and have offspring. Young males reject their mums in their adolescent years, despite all that these mothers have done for their sons, in order to separate and develop their own identities. Mothers are so incredibly righteous and awesome, nature had to synthesize a powerful chemical to lessen our bond.

The maternal connection is so Herculean that it can be superhuman. "Hysterical strength" is the extreme capacity for physical power a mother draws on when her child is in danger. This untamed display of strength, fueled by adrenaline, gave birth to the Marvel Comics character the Incredible Hulk. Jack Kirby, his creator, was inspired to father the viridescent superhero after he witnessed a woman lift her car to save her baby who was trapped underneath. The word "hysterical," of course, comes from the Greek word for "womb."

An underrepresented and unheralded example of another parental superpower is the self-control to shut our pie holes, step back, and allow our kids to learn from their own missteps and failures. Obstacles and mistakes have a negative reputation, but when we are faced with difficulty, we have the opportunity to prove our capabilities. Aristotle wrote, "It is expected that unexpected things should happen." Or, as my father always says, the problem is that we don't expect problems. You need failures and resilience to forge your identity as you separate from your parents.

One day at breakfast we were discussing the eighteen-year-long goodbye that serves as a person's launch pad toward independence. I noted that one random morning, the sound of me taking a bite of toast would repel you. There are many steps in the teenage evolutionary process. Young men need physical and psychological space from their mothers. You need to separate from me so you will not spend your prime breeding years living in my basement. I did love that special evening when you alerted me that the "Toast Bite of Teenage Independence" was finally heard. Except it wasn't the sound of toast that triggered your disgust; it was the sound of me chomping into a corn cob like Seabiscuit.*

I have to keep reminding myself that you have a juicy, developing teenage brain and I have a desiccated middle-aged brain. Your gray matter is vastly different from mine. The emotions you experience are more powerful because you have more neurons firing now than at any other time in your life. Between the ages of twelve and twenty-four, our brains develop and change in cataclysmically important and dramatic ways. In these dozen years of development, you obtain vital skills such as learning how to form and sustain friendships, how to navigate taking risks, how to become a citizen of sterling integrity, and, most

* The irritation that wells up inside certain people when they hear repetitive noises emanating from the mastication of those around them is called "misophonia." Your dad took a DNA test and besides being a Neanderthal of Greek and Irish origins, his genetic heritage indicates that he is congenitally sensitive to the sound of people chewing.

importantly, how to leave home. This inflates my heart and breaks my heart at the same time.

You're on your way to being a man of the world, and it's my job to prepare you in the best way I know how. I've turned to Stoic philosophers for guidance on what to tell you and also how to tell you. In the years AD 63 to 65, the retired Roman politician Seneca wrote a series of letters to a still-active younger colleague, containing a compendium of observations on subjects both mundane and elevated. *Letters from a Stoic* is one of the best and best-known texts of Stoic philosophy. The "epistolary form" of writing letters about philosophy was a well-established tradition among the Greeks and Romans. Through his letters, Seneca is attempting to convey and codify his philosophy.

I've always enjoyed writing letters to distant friends and family, and it suits me to write to you now. In our family we write letters and tape them to bedroom doors, slip them under pillows and into shoes. I always hide a letter in your father's travel bag so he can find it when unpacking. Some letters go through the post, some are left under the breakfast plate or in the refrigerator stuck to your orange juice. Sometimes I leave them in your goalie bag folded inside a skate. When I write you, I have time to think, compose my thoughts, and come up with astounding facts and dirty jokes you can use on your friends. You have time to digest it all at your leisure without needing to run away from my repulsive mastication.

I write you letters because I am confident that my words are better conveyed by my left hand than my mouth. I'm a gasbag, but I can edit a letter. I started writing to you before you were born, parenting for your future. I have siblings I can talk to when I need to fill in stories of our childhood. You are an only child, so these letters are a backup plan in case I get sawed in half by an amateur magician. I hope you will continue to read these letters to your kids long after my cremains are launched into the sky in a dazzling postmortem pyrotechnic display.

I am a black sheep who has raised a white sheep,

Mom

2

GET A LIFE PHILOSOPHY

Dear Cub,

The Romany community of Bulgaria has trained bears to dance for hundreds of years. It is a medieval tradition that lived on as a modern vestige of the Dark Ages. They raised the cubs in their homes and the bears lived in captivity with their owner's family. These were brown bears, *ursus arctos*, known in North America as the fierce grizzly bear.* The trained bears traveled throughout the region, entertaining Bulgarians wherever they went. The bears were taught to imitate celebrities, give massages to humans, and dance to a tambourine. They were plied with booze by their trainers and the bears were often drunk, but they were still able to perform their infamous dances while schnockered.

In 2007, Bulgaria was admitted to the European Union. Part of the price of admission was banning all dancing bear acts; treatment of the bears was rightfully deemed cruel and inhumane.

* The name "grizzly" may come from the fact that at a distance, its coat appears tipped in gray or silver—that is, grizzled. However, it may also derive from the word "grisly," meaning "horrifying."

The poor creatures had been captive their entire lives and their spirits had been broken. Some of the bears were alcoholics, addicted to strong spirits that weakened theirs.

Two animal rights organizations, Four Paws and the Brigitte Bardot Foundation, created a special refuge for retired dancing bears. The team at the bear sanctuary had a specialized task: they had to teach freedom to bears who had never been free. Their job was to teach bears to be bears.

The animal behavioral specialists retrained the bears, teaching them how to hibernate, how to hunt, how to have bear sexytime. Food was hidden around the sanctuary to reawaken the foraging instinct that had been trained out of them. The Dancing Bear Park became an ursine experiment in freedom. The bears had to relearn their independence one paw at a time.

Freedom was stressful and strenuous. The bears had to figure out how to live without the threat of the stick or the "treat" of a booze bottle. The sanctuary staff has had great success, but there are times when the bears struggle with the chaos of free will.

The difficulty of making their own choices causes pain. At these times the bears revert to the behavior that the rehabilitation staff were trying to get them to unlearn: when they see a human, they get up on their hind legs and dance a jig.

Free will is a challenge not just for retired dancing bears, but for all of us. When we're scared or threatened, we can fall back on bad habits, just like the bears. We don't sit up on our haunches and twirl, at least most of us don't, but we make bad choices, go along with ideas and plans we don't believe in, and close ourselves off to experience. Relying on unhelpful patterned responses lets laziness imprison us.

We all have a key to our own cages. Reading and educating yourself is a way to pick the lock. The only person standing between you and freedom is you. You are the boss of you; there is no one tethering you or muzzling you or making you dance the tarantella. It is up to you to make the most of your time here.

Jack, as a young man you're experiencing greater and greater freedom. You have the opportunity to take responsibility for yourself. You've always been mostly a perfect child, which has been sort of annoying. But I did notice that when we were shut up in quarantine, you went back to your old habit of letting your dirty boxers pile up in the middle of the floor. The good habit of washing your own laundry receded and, under stress, you reverted to being Pig-Pen.

Like the dancing bears of Bulgaria, humans sometimes fall back on bad habits in order to unburden themselves of some of life's stresses. With greater freedom comes the challenge of greater responsibility. This is why you need a philosophy of life. A life philosophy is not only about the big existential questions such as, How do I live a good life? Why are we here? How can I serve others? and, Who thought it was a good idea to give one-thousand-pound bears booze and make them shake their hind quarters?

A life philosophy is an attitude. It is your vision for your life. It is the direction you want to go, it is what you do with your freedom, it is your purpose. It is a framework to help you make decisions. It is the wisdom you'll refer to as you navigate the next eight decades.

Your life is a perishable good. Eighty years sounds like a long time, but it's just four thousand weeks. Squeeze what you can out of every day. Life is magnificent, then just okay, then amazing, then it is hard and it sucks a bit. But in between the awesome and the suck is the daily duty of living. Marvel at the awesome, and don't give up when it is hard. When it stinks, find a way to laugh. It will help you figure out how to make it suck less. This is your life, challenging, funny, and ordinary. The more it sucks, the more you need to suck in the amazing moments. Inhale, take it in. Honor your forty trillion cells that make you *you*. You are buzzing with life force, but we all need help in navigating the complexities of being a human.

Your philosophy for life is your operating manual. It will guide you through concrete questions, such as, What should I study in college? Is this the person I want to marry? How do I apologize after I screw up? What can I do to be of service? and How much should I duke the waiter? (At the very least 20 percent. You are descended from a long lineage of good tippers.) Answering these questions will help you answer the bigger ones, like, How can I be a good person? How can I live a meaningful life?

Philosophy in Greek means "love of wisdom." Wisdom is the ability to thrive in a complex world and make thoughtful, generous, and insightful decisions. The choices you make in everyday life are guided by your philosophy. Every day that you don't get up on your hind legs and dance like a Bulgarian bear is a win.

When I was in my late twenties, I joined some amateur archeologists on a dig at a historic Quaker estate at the eastern end of Long Island. These friends were adventurers, speechwriters, journalists, and celebrated documentary filmmakers. I fit right in with this illustrious group—I was an MTV VJ, mid-priced jeans model, and drugstore perfume pitchwoman, after all. We met through a book club and we have stayed close friends for decades. I'm grateful for their inspiration and guidance, and deeply thankful that they invited me to join that day's dig, excavating the estate's antique garbage pit.

Before getting down to the business of digging up pottery shards from the seventeenth century, we were given a tour of the manor. In a formal garden with a reflecting pool stood a row of marble heads. I was intrigued by the statuary, and the grand dame of the manor quizzed us on who they were. My friend Mary recognized the curly-headed visage of Marcus Aurelius, the last of the Five Good Emperors of Imperial Rome. I was deeply impressed. If Mary could clock the reflection of the Stoic philosopher-king with barely a glance, I knew I better bone up on my classical studies. Stupidity, ignorance, and envy are powerful motivators. The next day, I purchased the book *Meditations* by Marcus Aurelius, and it ignited my passion and my daily devotion to reading the Stoics.

I have been at it for nearly three decades, and I think I am a slightly better person for it. I don't get as angry or anxious and I don't get (or cause) *agita* as much as before. I've become steadier and more confident. A principal Stoic tenet is that we can't control what happens; we can only control how we respond. If something great happens, I can enjoy it without getting too caught up or attached to it. If what happens is bad, like my chronic ill health and intractable pain, I have strategies for dealing with them. I have learned acceptance and resilience.

I have kicked fear in the teeth, and I am living what I view as a good life. It is majestic and gnarly, and I am game for the next adventure. After living with a degenerative neurological disorder, after all my body has endured—chronic pain, neuropathy, impaired vision, and loss of smell—I am grateful for what I do have and what I can do. I don't lament what I can no longer do. I play to my strengths. Stoic principles have illuminated my self-confidence. I have inoculated myself from humiliation. In fact, if I ripped a deafening tugboat fart right now, I would excuse myself and carry on. If I have been thoughtless, I will ask for forgiveness and take actions to make it right.

Epictetus, one of the wisest and wittiest teachers who has ever drawn a breath, observed that everyone faces challenges and that a good life is within the grasp of all of us. He was born a slave, was savagely beaten by his master, and endured chronic pain and disability. I feel a deep connection to his wisdom. The simplicity and clarity of his ideology is transcendent: "If your choices are beautiful, so too, will you be." This is the thesis for my life. If I were the sort of person who writes and draws ideas on my body with needles and permanent ink, that thought would be my tramp stamp. Make good choices and you will make a good life.

There's a difference between a little-s stoic and capital-S Stoic philosophy. Little-s stoic means enduring hardships without complaining. Capital-S Stoicism isn't about keeping a stiff upper lip; it is about living a good and moral life. It's a classical Greek philosophy devised two millennia ago, but it reads as if the ink were still wet.* Stoic philosophy is a simple, clear road map to living a joyful, expressive life. It's shooting for the highest virtues, not suffering in silence. Stoicism isn't just for philosophers in an ivory tower, it's for everybody.

The three most renowned Stoic philosophers were:

Marcus Aurelius, the emperor-philosopher whose bust inspired me to learn about Stoicism;

Seneca, who was a powerful politician and a tutor to the Emperor Nero; and

Epictetus, who was born a slave and became one of the most revered scholars of classical Rome. He was maimed by his master, and his image always includes his crutch. His intelligence was so radiant that he was granted his freedom.

The ancient Stoic writers are long gone, but the concepts live on, in part because they were incorporated into Christian thought. There are two central goals that create the backbone of Stoicism: how to be a good person and how to live a good life.

My gateway book to Stoicism, Marcus Aurelius's *Meditations*, was actually his personal journal. He titled it "For Himself." I'd also advise you to keep a journal, for yourself, as a tool for self-reflection. It helps you to learn from your experiences, to forgive yourself when you have been a goon, and to prepare for a better day.

A journal is also a way to memorize valuable bits of wisdom. Writing them down helps fix them in your mind, and they will help guide you. "You become what you think about the most."

---

* The name "Stoicism" comes from the Greek word "stoa," or "porch." The founder of the Stoic school, Zeno of Citium, held meetings at the Stoa Poikile, the Painted Porch, a public space where anyone might come to discuss his ideas.

"Courage is knowing what not to fear." "Life gives to the giver and takes from the taker." I don't draw all my inspiration from dead white guys; that last one is from noted philosopher Reverend Run of Run-DMC.

One piece of wisdom I think about every day is another pearl from Epictetus, who believed that we can't control what happens, we can only control how we respond. This is known as the "dichotomy of control." If that rings a bell, it's because it is the kicker at the end of the Serenity Prayer, written by American theologian Reinhold Niebuhr in 1934. It has been recited at the end of every Alcoholics Anonymous meeting since 1935 and may be one of the most verbalized prayers in the world: "God grant me the serenity to accept the things I cannot change, the courage to change the things I can, and the wisdom to know the difference." Both the Stoics and Rev. Niebuhr agree that serenity is within you. It is a choice. Millions of recovering alcoholics can't be wrong.

The average person makes about thirty-five thousand choices every day. The ancient Romans used to flip a coin to make decisions. The "heads" side represented the emperor, who was also considered a god. If god came up, your choice was divinely blessed. For the ancients, "gastromancy" was a way of divining the future through stomach noises. "Tyromancy" means looking for omens in cheeses. Generations of humans have spent billions of dollars and countless hours on fortune tellers, horoscopes, tarot cards, Magic 8-Balls, and self-help books, all with the goal of discovering insight about themselves and how to live a good life. It may have been entertaining, but magic doesn't work, and research shows that self-help books can be tricky. The reward center of your brain lights up like the Christmas tree at Rockefeller Center just for buying the book, not for adapting new habits and making positive changes.

So, what does work? Reading the timeless classics and putting those ideas into action.

Methods of Divination and Fortune Telling

Alectomancy: Divining the future by interpreting the way a rooster pecks at grain.
Armomancy: Divination from the shoulders of animals.
Favomancy: Interpreting the way beans fall on the ground.
Hieromancy: Divination using entrails. Began in Mesopotamia and was used for millennia. In the nineteenth century, girls would fling herring guts at the wall to see the kind of man they would marry. A straight line meant a handsome, upright man and a squiggly shape meant short and ugly.
Moleosophy: Telling a person's fortune by moles. The mole on Robert DeNiro's right cheek indicates success and good luck.
Naevitology: Reading liver spots, carbuncles, and scars.
Nephomancy: Telling the future from the shape of clouds.
Nggam: A Cameroonian method of divination that interprets the movement of crabs or spiders.
Onomancy: Predicting the future based on your name.
Onychomancy: Divining by fingernails.
Parrot astrology: Trained parakeets tell your fortune by picking cards from a special deck.
Phrenology: Reading character and personality based on the shape of the skull. This was once classified as a science!
Pyromancy: The diviner observes flames and interprets the shapes to predict the future.

Snail divination: In Ireland, lovestruck girls would rise at dawn to examine snail trails, hoping they would spell the name of their true love. A black snail is unlucky, but a white snail brings good fortune.

Tasseography: Reading tea leaves, coffee grounds, or wine sediment.

* * *

For centuries, philosophers have tried to understand how we make decisions. In part it is because of the prior decisions we've made. The key is to make good decisions, and if you've been making bad decisions, to make better choices a new habit.

Twenty-four centuries later, the wisdom of the Stoic philosophers continues to help us make good decisions. Stoic philosophy is enduring. The art of living in our modern age can be enhanced by reflecting on the classics. The qualities that the study of philosophy offers you are profound; it creates a framework, a backbone of character. If you start to drift, it's a compass that shows you your direction and sets you back on course.

Stoic philosophy has taught me to tidy up my life and achieve my goals. I am squeezing the best out of myself and living a good life.

The wisdom you need to follow your own path is readily available to you. As Epictetus said, "it is all up to you and your way of thinking."

I endured years of fertility treatments to have you.
Don't be a helpless sack of organs,
Mum

—INTERLUDE—

Meet the Stoics

Stoicism originated in Athens around 300 BC with the work of Zeno of Citium. This school of philosophy, which taught that virtue is the only good, flourished throughout the Greco-Roman world. The writings of Seneca in about AD 64, the sayings of Epictetus from the early second century AD, and the journals of Emperor Marcus Aurelius from the period AD 161 to 180 are all important texts. Stoic teachings and ideas inspired Christian writers and Renaissance thinkers, and now we are in a new age of modern Stoicism.

Zeno, Seneca, Epictetus, and Marcus Aurelius—these four dazzling minds are your philosophical ancestors. They're your coaches in the game of life. They offer consolation when you are depressed, composure when you are anxious, and fortitude in your moments of weakness. The accessibility and simplicity of their Stoic wisdom transcends time, and you can be inspired by their lives as well as their philosophy.

Zeno of Citium. The founder of Stoicism, which was at first called "Zenoism." Zeno was not Greek; he hailed originally from Phoenicia, which was located along the coast of what is now Lebanon, Syria, and Israel. Like many of his fellows, he was a trader and traveled widely through the Mediterranean world. The Phoenicians traded a valuable commodity called Tyrian Purple, a special dye produced by mashing up thousands and thousands of sea snails. Zeno may well have been a merchant in Tyrian Purple, and he became a wealthy man.

On one trading voyage, Zeno was shipwrecked. He managed to make it to safety and washed up in Athens. While visiting a bookshop, he was struck by a biography of Aristotle and asked the shop owner where he could find similar men. Just at this time (so the story goes), the philosopher Crates happened to be walking by. Zeno became his pupil, and he began to develop a philosophy of his own. Supposedly, he remarked that "Now that I've suffered a shipwreck, I'm on a good journey," meaning that the unfortunate event had brought him to wisdom.

Zeno's teachings would come to be called Stoic because he and his pupils often gathered at the Stoa Poikile, the Painted Porch. His core belief was that humans should live in accordance with reason, and that was the only way to virtue. He urged his students to withdraw from emotions, tamp down their feelings, and become indifferent to pain and pleasure. I think this may explain the modern-day caricature of a Stoic as someone who represses all feelings.

Zeno's masterpiece was his *Republic*, which may have been a deliberate response to Plato's famous work of the same name. Although Zeno's book seems to have contained many worthy ideas, such as full equality of men and women, the first Stoic also seems to have been an insatiable libertine. Zeno's *Republic* advocates free love, masturbation, and prostitution, and while I feel these practices can be the subject of reasonable discussion, they are not primarily what draws me to Stoicism.

Seneca. This guy was a mover and a shaker. The middle son of minor Roman nobility far from the centers of power, he rose to amass great wealth, gain the ear of the Emperor Nero, and help rule the empire.

Lucius Annaeus Seneca the Younger, or just plain Seneca, was born in what is now Cordoba, Spain. His extremely ambitious father had high hopes for the lad. Seneca was packed off to Rome at the age of five with the idea that he would study and then rise in Roman politics.

Young Seneca was a sickly boy, possibly afflicted with asthma or tuberculosis or both, and many years of illness delayed his career. When he finally was able to take a seat in the Roman Senate, his speeches annoyed the Emperor Caligula so much that Seneca was ordered to commit suicide. He avoided that fate because Caligula was assured that he would die soon anyway.

Instead, Caligula was assassinated by his personal guards, and Seneca lived on. But the next emperor, Claudius, was no better for him. Messalina, the new empress, accused Seneca of an adulterous affair with Caligula's sister. This may have been a political ploy, but once again Seneca was sentenced to die. Luckily, the Senate commuted his punishment, and Seneca went into exile instead. He desperately wanted to return and began writing philosophy to ingratiate himself with Claudius.

Finally, Seneca was allowed to return to Rome and was appointed tutor to the imperial heir, Nero.

When Nero ascended to the throne, Seneca became his trusted advisor and helped rule the empire. As time went by, though, Seneca's influence waned and Nero became more erratic. The emperor even had his own mother, Agrippina, murdered.

Seneca began to withdraw from public life and spent his time writing his most famous work, *Letters from a Stoic*, messages of philosophical advice to a younger man. But years of political intrigue finally caught up with him. He was accused of plotting to kill Nero, and this time there was no escaping the sentence of suicide.

Seneca was a controversial figure in his own time. Though he insisted that poverty was no vice and wealth was no virtue, he amassed an enormous fortune and multiple estates. He forced conquered nobles to take on usurious loans, and he may have caused Boudicca's revolt in Britain by trying to squeeze the locals. He was even accused of orchestrating the murder of Agrippina, who was Seneca's great ally (he probably had nothing to do with it).

Yet Seneca's words still resonate with us because of the power of his writing and the clarity of his principles. He admitted that he didn't live up to his ideals, and who of us does? Although he considered himself a Stoic, he also rejected or reinterpreted some earlier Stoic ideas and took guidance from non-Stoic philosophers. His wide range of thought appeals to me. His resilience through political turmoil and numerous near-death experiences is inspirational. His writings influenced many early Christians, including Saint Augustine.

Seneca urged us to engage with the world because we have a duty to public service. At the same time, he recognized that different people engage the world in different ways. "What is required, you see, of any man is that he should be of use to other men—if possible, to many; failing that, to a few; failing that, to those nearest him; failing that, to himself." I also try to be of use—in big ways if I can, and in small ways if not.

Epictetus. The real name of this brilliant thinker and teacher is lost to us. "Epictetus" literally means "acquired," in the sense of property. He was born a slave, and it's unknown whether he was given this name or took it up himself. Epictetus walked with a limp, and one ancient author tells us that his leg was deliberately broken by his master.

His master, Epaphroditus, was a secretary to the Roman emperor Nero. Epictetus, though enslaved, was at the center of power and learning. He was given permission to study philosophy with a Roman senator, which was his introduction to Stoicism. He rose in stature as his knowledge and wisdom increased, but he remained subject to the tyranny of his owner.

Slavery was common in the ancient world. Roughly 40 percent of ancient Greeks were slaves, and up to 40 percent of the population of Italy were enslaved in Epictetus's time—comparable to the enslaved population of the Confederacy. It wasn't usual, but it was possible for Roman slaves to gain their freedom. At some point Epictetus either was set free or bought his freedom, and he began to teach philosophy himself.

When Emperor Domitian came to power in AD 81, he tried to rule as a tyrant and bypass the other parts of the Roman government such as the Senate. Many of those who opposed his high-handedness were Stoics, and in response, Domitian banished all "philosophers," including Epictetus.

Epictetus set up a school in Greece and became renowned as a teacher. Many powerful Romans came to hear him lecture, perhaps even the Emperor Hadrian. Emperor Marcus Aurelius considered himself a follower.

I find a lot of wisdom in Epictetus, but the most powerful of his maxims is the dichotomy of control: you can't control what happens; you can only control how you react to it. It is my bedrock belief and the principle that guides me through good times and bad.

As far as we know, Epictetus wrote nothing down. His teachings come to us through his student Arrian, who took notes on his conversations with the great thinker. Epictetus emphasized practical learning, a philosophy that is useful for life, and self-education, rather than abstract theory or book learning. I have chosen to honor my philosophical mentor with . . . a book.

Marcus Aurelius. At age sixteen, Roman noble Marcus Aurelius was placed in line of succession to be emperor. It was a usual practice at the time to steer the title not to a direct descendant but to a capable young man. Emperor Hadrian saw something in young Marcus, though he did not attain the throne until age forty.

As a youth, Marcus went through the standard education of a Roman aristocrat, which meant learning Greek and Latin rhetoric. At the urging of his painting teacher, he began to read philosophy. It's clear he was familiar with many writers, but he found special inspiration in Epictetus.

Marcus threw himself into living a simpler life than the others in the posh imperial household. He wore a rough cloak and slept on the ground until his mother, Domitia, finally convinced him to go back to bed.

The great work of his adulthood, *Meditations*, is a sort of diary packed full of thoughts and goals, reminders to do better and not become distracted by emotion and worldly things. He had a two-thousand-year head start on today's trend of journaling for self-improvement. In *Meditations*, Marcus Aurelius opened his writing by describing what each of his mentors taught him about being a good man, especially his mother. He wrote that Domitia gave him "piety and beneficence, and abstinence, not only from evil deeds, but even from evil thoughts; and further, simplicity in my way of living, far removed from the habits of the rich."

As emperor, Marcus Aurelius had many responsibilities and duties and was not especially fond of them. It seems he may not have even wanted to be emperor. But he felt he had to do his duty and try to improve the empire and the lives of its inhabitants. In *Meditations*, we see that even for the ruler of a mighty empire, with huge armies and vast wealth, it can be difficult to do the right thing. He inspires me every day to do my best according to my principles. It reassures me to know that if I don't quite live up to my own expectations, it will not result in a great famine or a crushing military defeat.

~

3

SAY NO TO THE PIGDOG

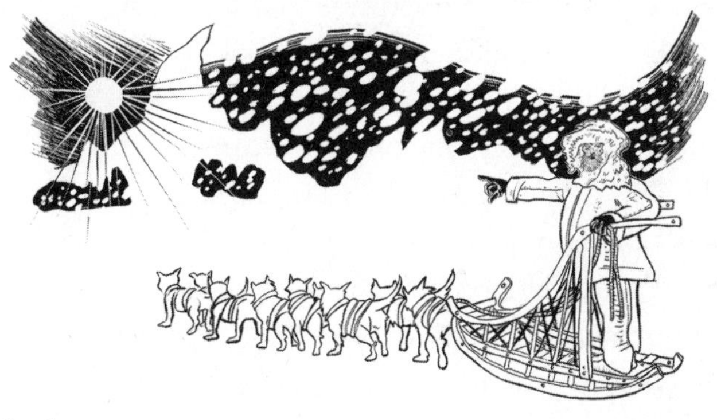

Dear Jack,

When Arctic explorer Peter Freuchen was dog-sledding across Greenland, he was buried by an avalanche. He crapped his snowsuit, but was it from fear? No. He fashioned a dagger from his own frozen feces and dug himself free from his icy almost-grave. His number 2 ingenuity saved his arse, and he went on to live an exceptionally vivid life as an adventurer, defeater of Nazis, and game show winner.*

* Great Dane Peter Freuchen lived a life full of astonishing escapades. The six-foot-seven-inch polymath later amputated his own frostbitten, gangrenous toes, though not with the same frozen knife he used to dig himself out of the snow. His books about his experiences with the indigenous peoples of Greenland were the basis for the Academy Award–winning film *Eskimo*. In World War II, he fought the Nazis, was caught, and was sentenced to death, but he escaped. After the war, he moved to the United States and won the grand prize on the US quiz show *The $64,000 Question*. His grandson by his first marriage, Peter Ittinuar, became the first member of the Inuit people to win election to the Canadian Parliament.

When Jean-Dominique Bauby endured a massive cerebral stroke and woke up weeks later completely paralyzed and speechless with the rare condition called locked-in syndrome, did he give up the ghost? No. When he realized that the only part of his body he could move was his right eyelid, did he shut it and wink hello to the grim reaper? No and no. He said yes to life and fulfilled his purpose as a husband, father, and journalist. He mentally composed and edited a book in his mind. Then, through a code that consisted solely of blinking his right eyelid, he dictated it one letter, one blink at a time. In this manner he wrote the masterful memoir that is his legacy, titled *The Diving Bell and the Butterfly*.

When Pascale Honore became paralyzed from the belt down as a result of a car accident, did she allow her disability to sideline her? No. She was an active mother of two surfing sons and she focused on her abilities—what she could do, not what she couldn't. She spent many adventurously happy days at the beach with her lads and their friends. Did she choose to simply sit in her wheelchair and smile while her sons rode the waves? No, she did not. Her dream of surfing became a reality when one of her sons' friends, a professional surfer named Tyron Swan, created a duct-tape harness and attached Pascale to his back. Did they "hang twenty" together and tandemly surf the waves with gorgeous grins gripping their faces? Yes.*

My fellow health care advocate Megan has been living with irritable bowel syndrome and Crohn's disease since she was two years old. Her serious medical conditions cause pain and impact every aspect of her life. Her conditions made an

* I have no way to know whether Tyron Swan has ever done this, but "hanging eleven" refers to a male surfing naked.

ostomy necessary. That's a surgery to redirect the contents of the intestine through a new opening in the stomach, called a "stoma." After the procedure, did she hide her stoma? No, she did not. She took on the nom de colostomy "Megan the Front Butt," and started a YouTube channel where she entertains and inspires. She fearlessly addresses the facts and shares information about living with a stoma. She is a role model to countless people and has been recognized for her advocacy. Her courage and good humor are a blazingly beautiful example of saying no to body shame and saying yes to living with vigor and dignity.

"Yes" and "no" are monosyllabic sentences. Pythagoras, the Greek philosopher, wrote that "the oldest, shortest words, yes and no, are those which require the most thought." These men and women of sterling integrity did not choose the easiest option. They chose to say yes to life and they took thoughtful, positive actions. They are all philosophers in my book, and because it is my book, philosophers they are.

I normally would advise you not to wager on a fart, but in Freuchen's case his gamble paid off. Rather than freezing his balls off, Freuchen made a chisel out of his excrement and hacked his way to freedom. Bauby was not defeated and against staggering odds he succeeded in expressing his life's purpose. Honore's life was a testament to overcoming barriers and an example of embracing life and duct tape. Megan the Front Butt proudly inspires us to not feel shame about our obstacles. These four valiant people are the personification of bravery. They did not quail in the face of adversity. Courage is developed by enduring the difficult times. As Seneca said, "Sometimes even to live is an act of courage."

I don't expect that you will grow up to be a hero, though I think you could become one if the need arose. I would prefer you not make a habit of crapping your pants, except in case of avalanche. We are not all called to great acts of heroism, but opportunities for daily acts of valor and courage are all around you. We all have a choice: be useful or useless. It is up to you to look for your shot to be useful: carrying groceries, holding the door, donating your time, buying a round, standing up for what is right, and being a mentor. Even the simple act of painting the benches in the Vesuvio Playground with your friends every spring is a contribution to the greater civic good. As Mother Teresa noted, "We all can't do great things, but we can all do small things with great love." I firmly believe it is a mistake to do nothing just because we can only do a little.

Opportunities for growth will not be presented in a perfect way; they will be challenging and messy. You will take a haymaker to the heart and get sucker punched by failure. It is going to sting and leave a mark, and most of us don't deal with pain very well. You will face frustration, fear, and anger, yet a steaming pile of failure can transform into the fragrant fertilizer that makes you grow, if you choose it. You are the sum of your choices. "We control our opinions, choices, desires, aversions, in a word, everything is our own doing," as Epictetus declared.

It is what you choose to do during your greatest struggles that shows you who you really are. To stagnate in mind or body is to surrender, to capitulate without terms. Action will dull fear. There is always something to do, even if that something is to prepare to accept what is inevitable and cannot be changed.

The Athenian statesman Demosthenes was orphaned at the age of seven. His guardians stole his inheritance, so as a young man, he took his fate into his own hands and retreated to a cave. He suffered from a stammer but was determined to make himself eloquent enough to win a court case against his guardians. He shaved half of his head so he would not be tempted to emerge from the cave with a half-mullet, half–cue ball. He practiced speaking with pebbles in his mouth to overcome his stammer and trained until he had become a confident and accomplished orator. (And he stayed in that cave until his hair grew back.) Faced with a dire situation, Demosthenes didn't complain or give up or focus on his victimization; he took action—and won his case through his oratory.

There is a spiritual equation that proposes that life is 10 percent what happens to us and 90 percent how we respond. You are not what has happened to you; you are what you have decided to become. Your habits, your attitude, and your choices, these decide your future. Every choice you make is a vote cast for the kind of person you will be. As Marcus Aurelius wrote, "At dawn, when you have trouble getting out of bed, tell yourself: 'I am rising to do the work of a human being.'"*

When you loll in bed after the alarm clock detonates, even though you have an early practice; or when you scroll through Instagram until your eyes bleed the night before you have a project due; or when you give in to that extra glimmering slice at Joe's Pizza on Carmine Street; you have revealed your weaker self to yourself. In Greek this is called "akrasia"—a lack of willpower that keeps us from doing what is good for us. But when you delay instant gratification to work toward higher goals, the Germans say you are overcoming your "innere schweinehund"—your "inner pigdog."

* The passage continues: "What do I have to complain about, if I'm going to do what I was born for—the things I was brought into the world to do? Or is this what I was created for? To huddle under the blankets and stay warm?—But it's nicer here . . . So were you born to feel 'nice'? Instead of doing things and experiencing them?"

German Compound Words

THE GERMAN LANGUAGE is full of colorful, cheeky compound words that express concepts that English does not. A rusty, beat-up bike is called a "drahtesel," which means "wire donkey." "Kummerspeck" translates to "grief bacon," meaning the extra pounds that chub you up after emotional overeating. It is livelier and more fun to say than "gunt" or "muffin top." Smoke-cured bacon is kept in a "kuhlschrank," or "cold cupboard" (a refrigerator). "Backpfeifengesicht" translates to the invaluable phrase, "face in need of a fist." Perhaps once we anglophones learn the pronunciation, it would be a great hockey term. Before fighting on the ice, players take off their hard gloves; in German, a glove is a "handschuh," or "hand shoe." You may have heard the word "schadenfreude," which means taking pleasure from another's suffering; you can use this after that face meets its much-needed fist. Your imagination is "das kopfkino" (a "head-cinema"). A bat is a "fledermaus," or "flutter mouse." Nipples are "brustwarzen," meaning "breast warts." "Der tagedieb" is a "day thief," a dawdler and layabout. Day thieves have given in to their innere schweinehund. If you have trouble remembering all this, you need "die eselbrucke," a "donkey bridge"—a memory aid for people with donkey brains.

* * *

Author, adventurer, and chef Anthony Bourdain remarked, "I understand there is a guy inside me who wants to lay in bed, smoke weed all day and watch cartoons and old movies. My whole life is a series of strategies to avoid and outwit that guy." "That guy" was Bourdain's innere schweinehund.

Your pigdog is the desire for immediate gratification. The pigdog values short-term rewards over long-term gains. In your beautiful, juicy brain, one part is devoted to plans and aspirations and keeps you committed and working toward your goals. Another part is tightly focused on the here and now. This is the devil pigdog on your shoulder. He nips and growls and squeals and oinks to keep you watching clips of the greatest hockey fights of all time when you should be practicing your French. When you overuse your smartphone or tablet, devices that have been engineered to engage the pigdog part of our brains, you give the porker the wheel.

The pigdog represents the lower, instinctual, and primal part of your gray matter, the limbic brain.* This is the most primordial part of your brain, which you share with reptiles, canines, and swine. The higher, more complex parts of your brain are what make you human.

Your appetites and instincts are not negative. They drive you to fulfill your very essential needs: to survive, thrive, mate, and reproduce. But the pigdog can be gluttonous and override your higher self. It's easier than ever to feed him—just think of how much junk entertainment and junk food there is, and how many bags of Flamin' Hot Cheetos I keep in the pantry. The trick is to take the wheel from the pigdog and pilot yourself toward your greater goals. This is in your control. You choose, not the pigdog. As Epictetus noted, it is all in your control, in your way of thinking.

There is an old story about a grandfather and his grandson. The grandfather tells his grandson that inside of him are two

* Your brain is actually a rosy hue when you are alive and using it. The tissue only turns gray after it is out of your head. So, it should really be called "pink matter." Your brain is also the only part of the body that named itself.

dogs. One of the dogs is mean, dangerous, and unpredictable, with sharp fangs and a taste for blood. The other dog is like our beloved cocker spaniel, Fredo. He is smart and disciplined. He's a good dog who protects his home and master. The mean dog is locked in a fight with the good dog. The grandson asks his grandpappy which dog will win. His granddad replies, "The one I feed the most."

When Walt Whitman wrote, "I am large, I contain multitudes," I don't think he was counting the folktale grandpa's good and bad dogs; Tony Bourdain's cannabis-smoking, cartoon-watching canis lupus; your puppy, Fredo; or our schweinehunds.

Your pigdog is guided by your choices and his jaws are snapping. How do you say no to your pigdog? How do you strengthen and nurture your good dog?

You can train your pigdog the same way you persuaded Fredo not to soak our carpets in urine. You focused on his positive behavior and reinforced his commendable conduct. Fredo was trained to exhibit positive attributes and was taught to prevent the negative ones from becoming habits. You taught him the basic tools to be a disciplined, well-mannered, and loyal cocker spaniel.

Your inner pigdog can be trained and guided by having an ethos, a vigorous philosophy of life that guides your choices and actions. We are what we repeatedly choose to do. Your habits, your attitude, and the decisions you make, make you. As my main man, the Stoic philosopher Epictetus, wrote two thousand years ago, "You are not your body and your hair style, but your capacity for choosing well. If your choices are beautiful, so too, will you be."

The entire point of evolution is for me to pass on my genes and my knowledge to you. If I get swallowed by a python, you will have Epictetus, Seneca, and Marcus Aurelius as your guides. They are my mentors. Their influence on my life is without measure. The most valuable advice I can pass on is to define your life's philosophy. As Marcus Aurelius urged, "Waste no more time arguing what a good man should be. Be one."

Train your pigdog. Make beautiful choices. You will make a beautiful life.

That's a fact, Jack,

Your überhebliche mutter

4

LOW-LEVEL HAPPINESS

Dear Jackhammer,

Isaac Newton, whom we can thank for creating calculus, also formulated the theory of gravity. While off from school due to a pandemic of bubonic plague in the early 1660s, young Isaac was reposing in the shade of his family's orchard. Legend has it that an apple fell from the tree and landed on his head. This was Newton's "aha" moment.* The apple inspired him to lay down the laws of gravity.

Archimedes was a scientist, inventor, and all-around genius madman who lived in the Greek city of Syracuse on the island of Sicily. His discoveries in mathematics are too numerous to list, but they laid the foundation for much of the homework sweated over by scholars through the millennia. The ingenious devices he created bear his name: The Archimedes screw is a simple device that's still used around the world to easily raise water to a higher level. The claw of Archimedes was a crane

* It could not have been his lightbulb moment, because fellow polymath Thomas Edison didn't patent that until 1879.

with a giant hook that could rip attacking ships out of the water. It's said that he invented a death ray (the Archimedes death ray, natch) that used mirrors to focus sunlight on enemy vessels, setting them on fire. Archimedes didn't just destroy warships; he designed one called the Syracusia. It was the largest ship built in antiquity, big enough for a gymnasium and a temple to Aphrodite. This guy seems like he was a barrel of monkeys. Really wise monkeys.

Archimedes's most famous exploit involved the crown of King Hiero. The monarch had supplied pure gold for the royal headgear but suspected that the metalsmiths might have pocketed some of the gold and substituted silver instead. He posed the problem to Archimedes, who pondered long and hard about how to supply a royal answer.

One day, as Archimedes slipped into his bath, he realized that the water level was rising; he was displacing an amount of water equal to the volume of his submerged body.* If the crown were placed in water and the rise in level was carefully measured, he would know the volume of the crown. If the crown displaced more water than the same amount of pure gold, that meant that some of the super-dense gold had been replaced with a less-dense metal. Archimedes was so excited by this realization that he jumped out of his bath and ran down the street stark naked, his frank and beans whistling in the wind, shouting "Eureka!"†

* It's not unusual for humans to figure something out in the bath or shower. We're alone in a quiet room; we're experiencing sensory deprivation that removes mental distraction. The warm water relaxes our tense muscles and increases dopamine to pleasure our overtaxed brains.

† "Eureka" is Greek for "I have found it!"

Newton had his apple, Archimedes had his bath, and my revelatory moment was inspired by a lowly mosquito bite.

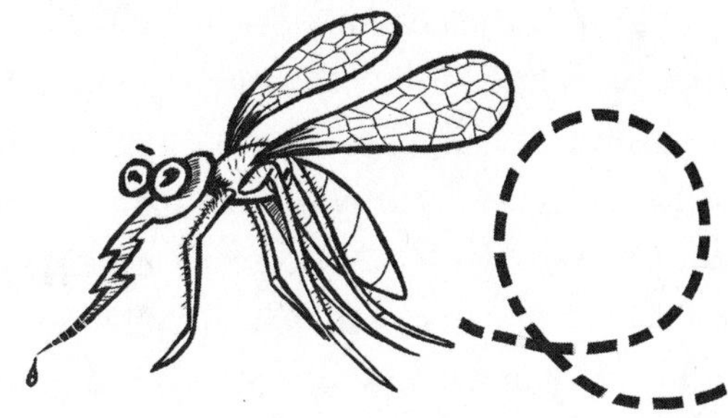

Last summer your father and I were invited to a swanky dinner party at the home of longtime family friends. It was a gorgeous evening in their lush Berkshire garden. After cocktails, I drew the long straw and had the great luck to be seated next to Yo-Yo Ma, the world-renowned cellist.

Mr. Ma is very easygoing and laid-back. He's smiley and warm and is a fountain of charisma. As we enjoyed casual hellos, he inquired about the large white patch I had stuck on my collarbone.

This ungainly accoutrement is the size of the jack of hearts, and I get asked about it quite frequently. It's definitely not a fashion choice; it supplies me with pain medication through my skin. It seems to provoke a strong reaction in people. The husband of one friend once asked me, "Why do you wear that? It's ugly." "Because I have to," I replied.

I was on a Poetry Walk with another friend, and he kept trying to adjust my shirt to cover it up. I asked, "What are you doing?" "I don't want people to see your patch," he replied. I am not ashamed of my medication. I'd wear it on my face if it gave me relief.

I explained to Mr. Ma that I have to wear the pain patch because of the severe nerve damage in my spinal column caused by sarcoidosis of the central nervous system. The inoperable lesion that blossomed in my spinal cord and my lower brain stem causes chronic, intractable pain. It's like an invisible parrot that is stabbing its claws into my shoulder and pecking my neck with its razor-blade beak. Mr. Ma took in my explanation and then warmly asked a question that has rarely been proposed to me. "How do you deal with living with chronic pain?"

The sun was setting, and buzzing insects took their cue to bombard us. As we swatted the mosquitoes, I had a eureka moment. When we get a mosquito bite, it itches. When we scratch the itch, we are creating a low-level pain sensation. The scraping distracts us from the vexing irritation of the bite. We are trading the annoyance of the relentless itch for a brief experience of mild pain, which we perceive as a relief.

Bite Me

Mosquitoes don't actually bite with teeth; they feed by sucking up liquids through their hollow noses. Male mosquitoes feed on plant nectar, which sounds delightful. Only female mosquitoes feed on humans. When they stick their sharp proboscis into your skin, they inject a chemical from their saliva to keep blood from clotting while they chug your life essence. This chemical causes a mild immune reaction. Your body releases histamine to help counter the foreign substance. Histamine causes the formation of an itchy bump, called a "wheal."

Our blood is full of the protein and amino acids they need to nourish their growing eggs, so not only are they irritating you but they're creating more mosquitoes to irritate future you. It would take 1.2 million mosquitoes, each sucking once, to completely drain the average body of blood. That's more likely to happen if your blood is type O; these airborne mini-vampires disfavor types A, B, and AB. Mosquitoes are the deadliest animals on the planet because of the diseases they spread, which include dengue fever, malaria, West Nile fever, filariasis, yellow fever, Zika, and elephantiasis. Five percent of all human deaths are mosquito-related.

These adaptive vermin will thrive in the most unlikely environments. In the London Underground, they have evolved so far from their aboveground cousins that they cannot interbreed, and they no longer hibernate in winter. Mosquitoes home in on their blood hosts by the scent of the carbon dioxide and lactic acid we produce, so a heavy breather is more likely to get swarmed. They're also attracted to nonenal odor, also known as "old person smell."

Mosquito "repellents" work by masking these smells. An effective home remedy is to set out a plate of Limburger cheese at your next garden party. The cheese emits an aroma similar to a very stinky human, which will divert the flying pests from your grateful guests.

* * *

In that moment I had a cataclysmic recognition. The way I manage living with high-level chronic pain is to jam as many low-level moments of happiness into my day as I can. Just as a small relieving scratch distracts me from an itchy wheal, I find that small moments of happiness distract me from high-level neuropathic pain.

On days when pain flares confine me to our home and I am roped to the sofa like Gulliver, I get a great dose of distraction from the pain in the pleasure of having a cup of tea and a biscuit, with old-school soul classics on the radio and the companionship of a great book on my lap. When I am up to it, I extract a higher-level dose of good vibes simply by walking in our neighborhood. Even when I am having a bad pain flare, I seek out positive interaction with neighbors and friends. They are an uplifting tonic for my soul.

I have found the way to distract myself from the unending agony of the evil phantom parrot that's pecking at my shoulder.

I give it a cracker.

My eureka moment didn't have me running down Litchfield Road in my birthday suit. I'm sure Yo-Yo Ma was grateful for that. I am grateful to him for helping me achieve the insight about how I manage to keep the pain-to-fun ratio leaning in my favor.

Christian philosopher and author C. S. Lewis advised, "Do not let your happiness depend on something you may lose." Well, I have lost my lavish good health, I've lost the ability to feel my feet and fingers, and the mobility to turn my head to the right. My head is cocked like a broken Pez dispenser. Too bad candy doesn't spring out of me when I'm in a pain flare.

I have a condition called allodynia, which is caused when your pain-processing system goes haywire. It is the experience in which a non-painful stimulus ignites an explosion of neuropathic pain. I can't tolerate my own hair strands touching my neck. I can't bear the graze of a collar or splashes of water from a shower. Like Archimedes, I appreciate a long soak in the tub, yet even a light breeze blowing on my neck can bring me to my knees. When air hurts, this is allodynia.

I've lost the simplicity of living a healthy, pain-free life, but I have gained a deep appreciation of how to squeeze the most out of my time here. Chronic pain has ratcheted up my gratitude for everyday joys. It has magnified my happiness in simply being alive.

Just as the classical Greeks understood that there are many ways to love, I believe there are many ways to connect to happiness. It cannot be confined to one definition or dimension. The word "happy" comes from the Norse word "happ," meaning lucky, favored by fortune, being in advantageous circumstances. As Seneca noted, "Luck is what happens when preparation meets opportunity." I believe there are opportunities to be happy all around us, and I am prepared to take them.

Words make me happy, like crackpot, wisenheimer, pickle, schnoz, and charley horse. I get a kick out of the fact that I have three friends named Happy. One of them is quite dour. I love the names Bill, George, Andrew, Lori, Lynn, Kate, Aida, Lizzie, Greg, Peg, John, and Jack. When I see those sets of letters on a page, they rearrange the chemicals in my brain and send a jolt to my heart, which lights up like I hit the jackpot on a slot machine. These names connect me to the people I love the most in the world.

Snow days make me happy. So does playing hooky with you and going out for French toast at our favorite scrappy diner, La Bonbonniere. I love that Marina and Gus have worked there for thirty-five years, and that ten years ago they bought this beloved greasy spoon from the former owner. When I saw Marina, who is an immigrant from Peru, and Gus, a Cypriot, do a conga line down Eighth Avenue, singing and banging pots to "Feliz Navidad" with Luis, the bus driver from Puerto Rico, I was inflated with pride and appreciation that we get them as our friends and neighbors. How did we get so lucky?

I'm happy to know that Louis Armstrong was so obsessed with a particular brand of laxative called Swiss Kriss that he signed his correspondence, "Swiss Kriss-ly Yours." It makes me happy to visit David at McNulty's Tea Shop. It is like a trip back in time to when your great-grandmother Chickie and great-aunt Gig lived in our neighborhood with their grandparents. David's shop has been on Christopher Street since 1890, and it is the most polite and positive 350 square feet in New York City. One time David said thank you to me thirty times during a brief transaction to purchase a box of PG Tips tea bags (I counted). He provides more than coffee and tea; he offers bags of happiness. I say a small prayer of gratitude for him whenever I put the kettle to boil.

Getting an email from my friend Sarah is like opening an exquisite present. Sarah has been living with amyotrophic lateral sclerosis, also known as ALS, for more than a decade. She composes her messages by using a special keyboard that responds to her eye movements. When she writes me an email it is a gift of her time. How can I ever thank her? My gratitude for our friendship is without measure. Letter by letter, operating a machine with her beautiful brown eyes, Sara asks how I am, how you are, and how your hockey season is going. Witnessing the way she navigates her life is like seeing a blueprint for happiness.

It's not the extraordinary strokes of good fortune that create sustainable happiness. A tequila-fueled night with Brad Pitt, visiting the pagan burial ground under the Vatican with our pal Father Andrew, cheering you as you got a shutout in the New York State Pee Wee Hockey Championship—these are moments of incandescent exuberance, but you can't pin down those fleeting experiences and capture that feeling forever. Bernard de Fontenelle, the French polymath, wrote that "a great obstacle to happiness is to expect too much happiness." The positive vibes evaporate quickly.

I remember visiting George Clooney in his trailer when he found out he was going to be the new Batman. I said, "This is amazing! You must be over the moon." I'll never forget what he said in return: "The best part is telling you guys, calling my friends and sharing the good news. But now, it's back to work." By his own estimation, he spent a decade acting in pilots that never went anywhere. He had learned to find happiness in the work, even if it never saw the light of day. He had learned that the unwavering love of friends would sustain him. He recognized and acknowledged that his dedication and tenacity brought him to this peak, and now life would move on. He understood that happiness is not in the fanfare of big moments; it is found in the small spaces in between and in sharing small moments with people you love.

My everyday happiness arises from focusing on small, inspiring daily occurrences, the joys of lovely, ordinary, everyday exchanges. These minor moments are always available to us, and they can add up to a major sense of well-being. Our gratitude for everyday blessings can rev up our baseline happiness. These non-monumental, low-level moments are the backbone of a grateful, happy life.

Paranoia is the belief that the whole world is conspiring *against* you. Well, pronoia is the belief that the world is conspiring *for* you. Perhaps life wants to bake you a cake, or freeze the pond with black ice that's perfect for skating, or deliver two down-on-their-luck jackasses to our farm just when we needed them most.

I am a coconspirator in pronoia. I look for ways to spread the vibe by doing small kindnesses for others. It makes people happy when you give an unexpected compliment, send a handwritten thank-you note, or duke the waiter a big tip. It makes you happy, too. You've surprised elderly neighbors by shoveling their walks. Every year, we sponsor foster kids to attend Camp Felix. When Mohammed, the corner fruit vendor, needs to answer the call of nature, we watch his cart. I'll bring him tea at the end of the day, and we crack jokes and exchange photos of our kids.

These non-monumental, low-level exchanges of happiness are the foundation of life. High-level happiness builds on this foundation to create fulfillment at a deeper, more meaningful and sustainable degree. Living in harmony with your life's purpose means using your strengths and gifts to aid the greater good.

My decades-long relationship with Ally from the Inner City Scholarship fund has mainlined happiness into both our lives. We were matched when she was in eighth grade. Ally shared her goal to go to college and study occupational therapy. We have kept our relationship going for nearly twenty-five years, and this week she sent me a photo of her doctorate diploma. Her radiant achievement is a gift to New York City and the world. I could not be more proud of her, and I've received such joy cheering her on through the decades.

High-level happiness is your flow, when you find your purpose and meaning—something to love, something to do, and something to look forward to. High-level happiness is a byproduct of being useful, being generous, and above all being kind. The ancient Greeks called this type of happiness "eudaimonia." It is more than just a pleasant feeling. It is the flourishing of a purposeful and meaningful life.

Happiness According to Aristotle

The noted philosopher Aristotle thought there were four levels of happiness:

1. Laetus, or happiness in a thing. You are happy because you have a book.
2. Felix, or happiness of comparison. You are happy because you have more books than your friend.
3. Beatitudo, or happiness from doing good. You are happy because you gave a book to your friend.
4. Sublime beatitudo, or supreme happiness. This is difficult to pin down, but it seems to be similar to eudaimonia. You are happy because books exist.

* * *

At your Pop Duffy's eightieth birthday party, he made a toast: "There are two important days in your life: the day you are born and the day you figure out why you were born." On the day you find your purpose, you are on your way to eudaimonia.

If you look for ways to increase your happiness, you will find them. I truly believe that every time I walk out the door, something fantastic could happen. I was driving with my dad when I was a teenager, and he remarked, "I wouldn't be surprised if the steering wheel I am holding would turn into solid gold right now." Aristotle would agree: your grandfather is a wise man, and a happy one.

You and your father are more pragmatic; you're amused by the Duffy family's cockeyed optimism. Whenever your Nan makes her famous linguini and clam sauce, Pa Duffy exclaims,

"Can you believe it? I got the pick of the litter. How did I ever get her to marry me? Isn't she a knockout?" You love to imitate him: "This coffee is the BEST I'VE EVER TASTED! Can you believe the paper cup it comes in?" I'm glad the Duffys offer you and your dad material to joke about and help maintain all your levels of happiness.

WE ARE HAPPY TO SERVE YOU

CLASSIC NEW YORK CITY DINERS were often owned by restaurateurs of Greek heritage. Realizing this, Holocaust survivor and paper cup entrepreneur Leslie Buck designed a vessel that catered to this demographic. For many decades, diner and street cart coffee has been served in a cup emblazoned with the message "WE ARE HAPPY TO SERVE YOU," featuring an image of a Greek vase called an amphora. The cup features the blue and white colors of the Greek flag; the blue represents the sky and sea, and the white represents clouds and waves. There is a decorative border in a geometric pattern called the "Greek key" or the "meander," which symbolizes infinity. The paper cup is called an anthora, which is a play on the word "amphora." The *New York Times* remarked that the anthora was "perhaps the most successful cup in history"; at the peak of its popularity, five hundred million were sold in a single year. Starbucks and diner owners from other countries have reduced the ubiquity of the cup, but it is still produced today in the original design and many variations, bringing small bursts of joy to nostalgic New Yorkers each time.

Ralph Waldo Emerson wrote, "It is one of the most beautiful compensations of life that no man can sincerely try to help another without helping himself." When you make a habit of practicing low-level acts of happiness, you will be lifted up and filled up in a way that even linguini and clam sauce never could achieve. I believe that doing small acts of good will bring you to experience eudaimonia, the flourishing state of happiness the Greeks so admired.

You need to find your own way to the art of happiness. It is not like a recipe I can hand down. You won't become happy by focusing on happiness; you will find it by focusing on what is good.

As Epictetus stated, "Our soul is dyed with the color of our thoughts." Go dye your soul with acts of kindness and happiness. It is all in your control, in your way of thinking.

Shine on, my beautiful son,

Your proud mum

5

THAT'S AMORE

Je t'aime, ti amo, ich liebe dich, eu te amo,
corazon, sagapo, my love, mi amore—

In my late twenties, I dated a guy named Whit, who was the lead singer of a popular heavy metal band. Whit was a bon vivant and a roisterer, a delightful mess of debauchery. I met him at a party when I was working at MTV. I left early to get my beauty rest. A friend showed me a photo of him taken later that evening—Whit was so drunk that his bandmates had to cart him back to his hotel room in a wheelchair. He had wet himself.

You may think this was a good reason for me to steer clear, and you'd be right. But Whit was enough of a good-time Charlie for two lifetimes, and I couldn't get enough. We once planned a tropical vacation to Bora Bora and met up after his world tour. The island was a palm-fringed, technicolor dream. We went out snorkeling with a guide we nicknamed Shark Boy. He warned us to stay away from the dark crevices in the coral reef because carnivorous moray eels lurked there. Whit immediately swam over and pretended to hump a moray hidey-hole. When Shark Boy gave us frozen bait to feed the reef sharks, I gingerly held the fish sticks as they grabbed the bait from my hand. Whit clenched a snapper between his butt cheeks, to make me laugh. That's A-moray!

I was at his house in Los Angeles once and he came home hammered and happy. He'd just played a show and it had gone great. "Baby, I love you," he said. "That's swell, Whit, but why do you only say you *love* me when you're wasted? Why don't you say it when you're normal?" "'Cause *normally* . . . you're not that cool," he drawled. I laughed until I cried. I still laugh when I think of it.

Since your father is named John and not Whit, you're aware that that relationship came to an end. I stayed with Whit way too long, and the hilarity of that statement was one of the reasons.

I still love Whit; he is a human cyclone of charm and good vibes. My confusion at the time was that I didn't understand how I loved him.

There is a performative side of parenting in which adults present only their best attributes to their children. We project these personas that parents are upstanding citizens with a pristine past. We don't share the screwups, the reckless shenanigans, or the spirited jackassery. These misadventures are probably what you need to hear about the most. Parents are not perfect; we fail spectacularly and we all have tales of juvenile buffoonery. Yes, even me. I know that will come as a surprise.

You are just about to emerge into the part of your life where you'll experience romantic relationships. I do want you to be a gentleman and I want you to treat your partners with respect. I don't want you to have a narrow scope of references that limits you in love. The soft spot of your skull solidified years ago, but your soul is still pliable. The cement is still wet. You're at an impressionable time of life, and I want you to know that there are a lot of ways to love.

For me, it was a late-in-life, overdue revelation when I realized that there is more than one definition for love. The English language has only one word for many emotions. We have an impoverished language. We casually toss the word around like parmesan on spaghetti. I love you, I love time alone with a book, I love buying used prostheses as gifts for your father. I love the New York Rangers, I love to make needlepoint whoopie cushion covers, I love our jackasses. Those are all very different feelings covered by one four-letter word. It is like lumping together the Carolina Reaper with the Ghost with the Sweet Bell and calling them all peppers.

When I learned that the ancient Greeks had many words to describe love, I gained a way to describe my feelings more fully. This refined taxonomy encompasses an enormous range of varying emotions, relations, and connections. The types of love include:

Eros: sexual passion
Philia: deep friendship and affection
Ludos: playful love
Pragma: enduring love
Philautia: love of self, the romance of solitude
Agape: love for everyone, selfless love

Throughout the ages, from the moment our monkey hearts began beating in our hairy chests, our minds have grappled with the eternal question, What is love? The first place I go for answers is the Stoics. Epictetus said, "Whoever then understands what is good, can also know how to love." But the enormousness of the inquiry calls for additional perspectives. My other revered philosopher, Frank Sinatra, claims that "Love is lovelier the second time around." (Could that be pragma?) The Reverend Al Green sings of "Love and Happiness." (Possibly philia?) Prince wrote that love makes you "Somebody's Somebody." (This is Prince, so that's probably eros.) Lennon and McCartney summed it up by singing "All You Need Is Love." (Definitely agape.)

Over the last millennium, all these varieties of emotion have been collapsed into one mythical concept of romantic love, where one person is your amorous Swiss army knife. That's a lot of pressure to put on someone, especially the one person you love the most. The idea of romantic love is a medieval construct from the days when people thought the world was flat, were convinced that witches kept male genitalia in nests as pets, believed that evil demons lived in brussels sprouts, and considered blowing smoke up your butt to be the latest in medical science.

Medieval Love and Marriage

In the Middle Ages, people bathed once every twelve months, usually in May, and not for very long, either—excessive bathing was thought to cause fatness and feebleness. Weddings were held in June so everyone present would be less smelly than at other times of year. The bride carried a bouquet anyway, to mask the stink emanated by those who hadn't taken the annual plunge.

You didn't have to get married in church; the ceremony could take place outside the church door, in a pub, or even in bed. You didn't even need a priest or witnesses, even after marriage was declared a Christian sacrament in the twelfth century. As long as two people agreed they were married, they were married.

Weddings often included a gift from husband to his wife, and it seems some young lads would give lasses a little trinket to trick them into thinking they were wed, and they'd then have sex, then deny they were married. The only people who ever married for love were those with few worldly possessions, and even lower-class parents would arrange marriages for their children.

Christians were officially prohibited from divorcing, but in parts of Germany, if the marriage didn't work out, the couple could attempt a divorce by combat. The husband, with a club in one hand and the other tied behind his back, stood in a waist-deep hole. The wife, armed with rocks in a cloth sling, danced around the edge, and they both tried to beat each other's brains out. If the woman won, the man was executed. If the man won, the woman was buried alive. 'Til death do them part.

⁂ ⁂ ⁂

In the twenty-first century, scientists have created an artificial heart. Our friend Bernadette has a pig valve in her ticker. Your aunt received a jawbone from a cadaver, our friend Pete got a lung transplant, and that lady who got her face clawed off by a chimp had a new one sewn on. Medicine has made great advances. It's time we update our ideas about love, too.

I reject the term "soul mate." The ancient Greeks wouldn't have understood the primitive way we use the term. You have one soul, but you'll have romantic partners, good friends, teammates, roommates, and many other mates. You will love them all in many different ways.

The types of love the Greeks knew will open a door to your having better relationships. Maybe you're not ready for the sexy-Prince-soundtrack kind of love, and if you are, please don't tell me. But all your relationships with your friends, your family, your mentors, and your girlfriends will be strengthened by understanding the many forms of love. Let's take a deeper look at their taxonomy:

> **Eros** was the Greek god of love and fertility. He wasn't the cutesy, chubby Cupid you see on greeting cards. Eros represented sexual desire and passion—an erotic loss of control, which was worrying to the Greeks. Today, we often view this as a key part of romantic relationships, and it's nothing to fear. You will experience kisses so intoxicating your eyes will roll back in your head so far that you will get a glimpse of your own brain. Your glands will shoot a bottle rocket to your nether regions. Robin Williams said that "God gave man a brain and a penis, and only enough blood to run one at a time." Lust is nature's trick to make us make more people.

Passion can happen at any age, but you will never have as many neurons firing in your brain as you will from the ages of thirteen to twenty-four. This is why teenagers feel things with an intensity that could be gauged by a seismometer. Young love is an affliction of youth, like cultivating a bumper crop of zits, going to water parks, and updating your mother's phone.

Philia, or friendship. The Greeks considered friendship a higher, more virtuous form of love than the passion of eros. At your school, you call your classmates "brothers," and your love for your brothers is philia. The word also describes the comradeship of men who have fought together in battle. Perhaps it applies to your relationship with your scrappy hockey teammates? Society doesn't recognize friendship as an institution like marriage or domestic partnership, but some of the longest, strongest relationships will be philiac.

Ludos is playful, jokey, flirty. Ludic love is kidding around with friends. It's the jokes and pranks we play on people we care for, like the times we say goodbye to your uncle George and aunt Amal after our summer visits to the lake. You've spent every summer of your life with George, and every time we leave, we are a bit sad in our hearts to say goodbye. That jumpy, longing feeling evaporates when we get to the airport and realize that George and Amal have filled our luggage with gravel and heavy, ugly bronze statues left over from the previous owner of the house. These jokes are ways we show affection. That's ludic love. Ludos can help form deep bonds; Plato said, "You can discover more about a person in an hour of play than in a year of conversation." Ludos is what I had with Whit.

Pragma is about commitment. It's realistic and compromising. In couples, it guarantees stability for the family. Pragmatic love is an act of reciprocity, a sense of sharing with and giving to your partner. It's the shorthand of knowing that your partner is working hard and would really appreciate a turkey BLT. Philosopher Erich Fromm wrote about the distinction between falling in love and what he called standing in love. We spend so much energy on the fall—the chase—and the dopamine and adrenaline hit from taking risks to pursue a partner. In other words, we obsess on eros. Fromm said we should focus more on standing in love, on giving love rather than receiving it. When you're standing in love, you're ready to catch your partner if they fall.* Pragma can consist of grand, thoughtful gestures, like your father planning a vacation in our favorite spot or surprising me with his beloved grandmother's ring. Pragma is also when he gets up at the crack of dawn on snowy winter mornings to walk the dog and leaves me piping hot coffee just the way I like it on the nightstand.

Pragma also describes the love of a parent for a child. We make compromises and give as much as we can, not from duty but from love. I never minded the

* When we're falling in love, it's said that we're "head over heels"—but aren't we normally head over heels? This sounds like pragma to me—standing in love. Heels over head would be Eros.

chilblains I suffered from spending years shivering at ice rinks while you practiced and played hockey.

Philautia means self-love, and get your mind out of the gutter. When you love and admire the person you are, and feel secure in yourself, you will have a limitless supply of love to give. Conversely, if you wallow in self-loathing, you will have little love to share with others. As Aristotle said, "All friendly feelings for others are extensions of a man's feelings for himself." When you know what makes you happy, you can extend happiness to other people. There's a humility to philautia; it's about accepting weaknesses and imperfections. It's self-compassion. Philautia is the opposite of posting selfies on Instagram using a dozen filters.

Agape, or selfless love, is altruistic and offered to all creatures. It's love given without expectation or obligation. It balances our desire to be loved with our generosity of spirit. Mary O'Connor, a waitress at one of my favorite restaurants, Neary's, overheard a regular patron talking about his need for a kidney transplant. She was so moved that she donated her own. Her kidney was too small for the customer, so it was given to another recipient. It didn't help her customer directly, but her action helped him move up the list for a new kidney. The wife of the gentleman who got Mary's kidney was so awed by her selfless gesture that she, too, became a kidney donor. A further eight strangers were inspired by the story to donate a kidney of their own. Mary's agape helped save the lives of eleven people.

> But you don't have to undergo surgery to express agape. When we visited Naples, the fellow in line ahead of us at the Gran Caffè Gambrinus ordered a "caffe sospeso." We inquired of the barista what that might be, and he explained that people often bought a "suspended coffee"—they paid for a cup that would be drunk by somebody who couldn't afford one. Agape is what moves you to make lunch for senior citizens in your dining hall at school and read to little kids at the library.

In our culture, "love" means finding that one special romantic partner, falling madly in love, and living a fairy-tale life together. I think you've learned by now that fairy tales are malarkey, despite me hiding under your bed pretending to be a troll. Some of us are incredibly demanding and particular about our Starbucks order, the thread count of our sheets, and the type of milk we drink—skim, 2 percent, oat, soy? Yet when it comes to love, it's just supposed to magically happen on some enchanted evening, as if we were at the mercy of the Hogwarts Sorting Hat.

Why do we devote our time to the search for the perfect romantic partner? We should be awake to the many kinds of love. You are responsible for your own fulfillment. No one will provide it for you. The idea of marrying for love is a recent one, invented in the Middle Ages to occupy the thoughts of randy courtiers and louche ladies-in-waiting. For most of human history, marriages were arranged. Your family married you off to your neighbor so when the parents croaked, you could combine their two small farms into one big new one. I guess that's a happily-ever-after?

You don't have to be limited by medieval notions of love. Nor do you have to be involved in purely transactional matches.

There's no reason to despair. I hope you will fall passionately for someone—and that you also experience other forms of love. You may have sex with someone you like, and you may never have sex with someone you love. It's tricky like that.

I'd like to pause and spare a thought for the great philosopher Plato, whose name lives on in the term "platonic love," meaning no boning. It's come to mean a friendzone situation, where you're probably not going to have sex with that person. Actually, platonic love celebrates the deeper connections possible through pragma and other non-eros types of love. Let us remember him for firing the starting pistol at the beginning of Western philosophy. Let's honor him for his contributions to history, not pity him for something lacking with regard to the commingling of the male and female nectars.

Erase, Wite-Out, Alt-Ctrl-Del the idea of finding one perfect partner. Everybody has a wish list of what they want in another person, and at the top of the list is someone who's funny. But everyone thinks that they're funny. It's a heavy lift to ask one person to satisfy not only our desire for eros and philia, but also to keep you rolling on the floor laughing with milk coming out of your nose. It's unfair and off-balance and unrealistic to burden yourself and someone else with those expectations.

A limited vocabulary stunts your definition of love, but cracking the *thesaurus de amor* removes those constraints. A relationship can encompass all kinds of love. It can begin in eros or philia or ludos, and through philautia, grow into steady, standing-in-love pragma. This gives us the ability to express agape. It is a gift of your Hellenic heritage that you can adopt this new language of love and be fluent in all six definitions. You will not feel madly, passionately, crazily in love with your partner for your whole life, the same way you don't explode with gratitude for every breath you take. Time blunts the edges. You won't do a rhumba of happiness every time you walk your kid to school. Love and gratitude will grow into a more steady and easy presence. You will get back to the business of living your life. (That said, I admit to still getting caught in fits of delirious passion for your father, to his great annoyance.)

The majority of my friends are single and vividly happy. Some have been married and have been there, done that. Others never wanted a partner for life. A few had short marriages and they did not breed in captivity. Leopoldina is a merry widow. She had a great marriage, and her life of sexy solitude is punctuated by visits from her younger boyfriend. It suits her for now. For others, they are content to see what time will bring. Love has its own chronology.

We don't have a finite, limited reserve of love. It's a vast reservoir that constantly refills and never empties. Practicing love engenders more love. We aren't limited to loving one mythical soulmate. As one of your wise godmothers, Candace Bushnell, wrote, "One has to become one's own soulmate, you have to have a good relationship with yourself. You go everywhere with yourself." We are super-spreaders of love, with so much to share and so much to receive.

Being single doesn't limit the love in your life. You can be an alloparent and help raise a child who isn't yours. You can love an animal and be loved in return. You can be a mentor and help guide a young person to maturity.*

* The word "mentor" is a reference to Athena, the Greek goddess of wisdom. In Homer's Odyssey, she visited Odysseus's son, Telemachus, disguised as a man called Mentor. It was Mentor's advice that Telemachus should stand against his mother's suitors and find out what happened to his missing father.

My friend Genevieve made the decision that she would not have children of her own, but she wanted children in her life. She volunteered at a group home for kids. After work, she would read them books and tuck them in. One evening it struck her that some of the kids didn't have pajamas. Sometimes, when a kid is removed from a rough situation, the cops or social workers take a big plastic bag and throw stuff in fast. Pajamas aren't a priority. Most kids slept in the clothes they wore all day. Genevieve recalled the comfort and secure feelings she experienced when she was wearing her favorite PJs as her mum tucked her in, and she set a goal. Each year more than four hundred thousand kids cycle through social service care, so she aimed to collect and distribute one million sets of pajamas. She has far exceeded her goal: she's given out 6.5 million pairs of PJs through her Pajama Program.

I was a late bloomer and was single for much of my young life. When I was fourteen years old, my friend Annunziata from the cheerleading squad had a steady guy. She was always complaining: "If he doesn't send me flowers and candy for Valentine's Day, that's it!" She was acting like a nagging fishwife in our freshman year of high school. I wasn't in a rush to take on that role.

Saint Valentine

Bishop Valentinus was a third-century priest who was martyred for his Christian beliefs. He would have lost his head to discover he has become the avatar of romantic love; in life, he ministered to persecuted Christians, not lovesick teens, and was beheaded for his troubles. In 1382

Geoffrey Chaucer wrote a poem called "The Parliament of Foules," describing Valentine's feast day on February 14 as a time for birds and people to choose their mates. From then on, Saint Valentine's reputation as a healer of epileptic seizures was overshadowed, and Saint Valentine's Day was turned into an opportunity for people to exchange red cardboard boxes of Russell Stover chocolates. Pieces of his body have been dispersed around the world as holy relics, and his skull, crowned with flowers, can be seen in the Basilica of Santa Maria in Rome. Like many saints, he has had a busy afterlife—he is the patron of beekeepers, epilepsy, fainting, traveling, the plague, and, of course, lovers and happy marriages.

* * *

I didn't really date until college, and not much in the years afterward. It didn't suit me. I spent many years being single. I got pressure from friends and family over this, but I shrugged it off. I wasn't in a race. Some friends would still try to fix me up with dates, and once I was invited to a dinner party at which "Richard" would be my companion. I showed up late and the only empty seat available at the table was across from . . . Richard Gere. I thought, "You are so out of my league, and why didn't she warn me?"

I never felt lonely because I had the love of my best friends, which I continue to treasure. I always felt such love, support, and affection from them. Their philia comforted me. I was happy with what I was doing with my life. I liked being alone. I liked my own company. I was comfortable with philautia. I volunteered at the nursing home; I had agape. When I didn't have a boyfriend, I still had a lot of love in my life. I gratefully declined five marriage proposals; looking back, it would have been more graceful not to have cracked up while I was turning the guys down, but I don't regret saying no.

When I did start dating more in earnest, my preference was for complete knuckleheads. One guy dressed up as Ernest Borgnine to take me on a date. Another bought me a pair of size eighteen Converse high tops as a Christmas present. I wore them over my shoes on our next date.

I dated one guy for way too long because I loved how sweet he was to little old ladies, and that he called old men "Boss" with reverence and dignity. We project qualities on our *objet d'amour*, so it feels like we didn't make a mistake. I'm a generally upstanding citizen and I assumed he was too. I thought he was a film producer, but after a year with him I came to realize he might actually be a counterfeiter.

With regard to your father, I find it hard to write about him; it's difficult to paint a factual portrait of a man whom nobody seems to dislike. The power of his charm bathes me in warmth, as do his looks of affection. Your father's face is my favorite view on Earth. Making him laugh until he cries is a victory I strive for every day. Being married to him is kind of old school, a bit like joining the Shriners; we have a lot of fun and try to put more good into the world, but we don't have to wear the fezes or ride on adult tricycles. I am glad you are half John Fortune Lambros.

Your father fascinates me. Every day I feel like Jane Goodall, but instead of a regal aristocratic primatologist, I am a Jersey-born former MTV VJ who is a bit too fond of pie. Instead of observing the dominant male in a troop of chimpanzees in the forests of Tanzania, I am marveling at your father's easy confidence from across a book-filled room. He is an Ivy League, Park Avenue blue blood. Your dad and I have a mixed marriage—he's all class and I'm all sass. I keep a tally of things your dad has never done: swum in an above-ground pool, shopped at a mall, set an L. L. Bean Blucher shoe inside an amusement park or carnival. I am the former Queen of the Coney Island Mermaid Parade . . . your dad has never been to a parade. I am a hypergamist: I married up.

Marriage is a traditional institution, and being married to John Fortune Lambros feels extremely traditional, like being in the Social Register blue book—which your father is. I always feel on thin ice with him. I've got one foot on a banana peel and one out the door. At the beginning of a relationship, you present a perfect impersonation of the best version of yourself, and as time goes on you let the imperfections out. Once we were driving to a friend's house, and I was giving directions. Your dad missed the turn. Steam came out of my ears, and I growled, "I . . . SAID . . . TURN . . . RIGHT." He said, "Put the mask back on, I never want to see the real you again." Your father likes when I do ridiculous things to make him laugh, but I secretly worry that someday I'll go too far and be voted off the family. I'm still finding my way. My dad told me that the first fifty years of marriage are the hardest.

Now that I've been married to your dad for two decades, I'm not dating as much. I still think I have penetrating insight and wisdom to offer you: romantic love is like a can of mixed nuts. Sometimes there are delicious, salty snacks in there, sometimes a snake jumps out.

In the end, Jack, we're all just bags of chemicals. From your conception to this day, billions of biological reactions have made you who you are. The mechanisms that helped shape you were determined by evolution, and the point of evolution is reproduction, not finding a soulmate. This is one reason so many people make bad choices in partners—they're being helplessly driven by hormones. Oxytocin urges us to bond with others—our lovers, our friends, our children, and even our pets. Dopamine causes us pleasure in the relationship. The rush of ecstasy that sex gives is ignited by endorphins.

We're not marionettes, dancing when these chemicals tug on the strings. I believe that when we are conscious and thoughtful about how we love, these hormones are the effect of our behavior, not the cause.

You can magnify the love of philia by doing something brotherly with your friends. Amplify your ludos by going to school dances. Practice philautia by spending a quiet afternoon walking the dog. The narrow interpretation of love will cause suffering, but when you look at love in all its forms, you will feel a radiant abundance of joy.

Love yourself, that is the best foundation. When you love yourself, you gain confidence, you will have faith in yourself, and you will have love to share with others. When you can make yourself happy, you will have the capability to make others happy. The expansive beauty of the classical Greek definitions of love inspires us to embrace the various forms of it rather than focusing on the pursuit of romance. When our hearts are open and expanded, we become fire hoses of compassion and all forms of love.

Saint Thomas Aquinas wrote that "the things we love tell us who we are." From reading this letter, you can tell I love spicy food, chimps, Frank Sinatra, and most of all you and your dad.

Jack, at the end of your life, when you ask yourself what you have done, the best and only answer is love.

Your loving mum

6

INVICTUS

Dear Jack,

One of my favorite things to do when we travel is hit up local pharmacies, stationers, and grocery stores for mementos. Duty free? Not for me. I like bringing home toothpaste, dishwashing soap, tea bags, and notebooks, the kind of staples we use every day, to remind us of our family trips. I drink the Jamaican Caribbean Dreams instant ginger tea sachets like I've entered a ginger tea drinking contest. We have hot sauce from multiple countries on our kitchen counter. My favorite bath soap is from the Florentine outfit Santa Maria Novella, the oldest pharmacy in the world, founded by monks in 1612. I like bringing home small utilitarian objects, while some people hoover through the luxury boutiques as if they are playing with Monopoly money. We've even been on a beach vacation with friends when a stray dog weaseled his way into their hearts, and they arranged at great expense to transport the four-legged souvenir home as a new member of their family.

I recently read about another family who fell in love and bought a dog while on vacation. They returned to their home in

Yunnan Province, China, and raised their beloved pet for two years. The pup grew at a ferocious rate, devouring a box of fruit and two buckets of noodles every day. He attained a tremendous size and started to look like a different animal entirely. When he began walking on his hind legs, the startled family finally realized that they had been raising, not a 250-pound Tibetan mastiff as they had believed, but a rare Asiatic black bear, which they were now very eager to get rid of. "I am a little scared of bears," the mother remarked.

I was struck by the fact that she wasn't afraid of this enormous ravening beast when she thought it was a dog. It lived in their home and she thought of it as an affectionate, snuggly companion. As Marcus Aurelius wrote, "All is as thinking makes it so." She only became scared when she realized it was a bear in dog's clothing.

We are a rescue-dog family, but if this story doesn't convince you that shady puppy vendors are questionable, that you could pay for a dog and come home with a wild beast, well, then you are on your own.

Our family's farm in a rural corner of Connecticut is lousy with American black bears. Every time an unwelcome visitor starts kicking up a ruckus in a more populated area, the good people at Environmental Protection relocate the unruly ursine to our environs. Our neighborhood is like a bear rehab. I'm always thrilled to view these magnificent animals in the woods, but from afar.

The Miracle of the Bear

I LOVE THAT the Catholic faith has a patron saint for nearly everything, and the patron of bears is Saint Corbinian. He was a hermit who was determined to make a pilgrimage to Rome. On the journey, he was ambushed by a bear, which ate his pack horse. With a stoic sangfroid, he made the bear carry his luggage to the Holy City. Upon arrival, he freed the bear, which returned to the wild. I'm not sure this is a story that would gladden the hearts of Catholic bears, but the ways of the church are mysterious.

* * *

Last fall I was strolling down our road in the hills near our farm, returning home from a long walk. It was a beautiful day and the gentle pace in nature was helping me get over a pain flare. A car approached me from the opposite direction and came to a stop. "There's a bear down there, but don't worry, it's only a cub," the driver said. I thanked him and walked on, being sure to make noise as I went, so as not to startle the young bear with my looming presence.

A couple hundred yards down the road, I heard rustling in the forest on my right and I suddenly realized with great clarity that I didn't want to encounter a bear of any age or size. Just as I was having my epiphany, the cub emerged from the trees about twenty feet away. He looked plenty big enough to me—not full grown, but more of a yearling than a cute little Teddy cub. Roughly a young Danny DeVito–size bear.

I had studied up on what to do, as I'd always known there was a chance that I might encounter one up close. I made myself "big" by raising my arms over my head. I didn't look the cub in the eyes. I spoke in a calm and even tone. I don't remember what exactly I said, but it must have greatly angered him, because he let out a bowel-evacuatingly scary growl and charged me. He didn't bite or claw me, but he did ram me with his shoulder as he went by, before turning and running back into the woods.

The blow caused me to stagger back a few steps, and I was lucky to stay on my feet, as I'm not very steady to begin with. I didn't know what to do. At this point I heard a crashing noise in the forest to my left, and I recalled that a bear cub is never far from its mother. I was now in the proverbial worst place in the woods: between a mother bear and her cub.

I couldn't see the mama yet, but I knew enough not to turn and leg it, because the bears could move faster than me, and there was no elderly person or small child nearby for me to outrun. I moved away slowly, still babbling nonsense in what I hoped was a calm tone. I took careful steps backward, praying that I wouldn't trip and fall.

The mama bear came charging out of the forest and ran across the road and into the woods where the cub had gone. I paused for a bit, wondering whether it was safe to reverse course and head home. The mama bear had other ideas. She came back out of the woods and began patrolling back and forth, blocking my way. She was big, maybe two hundred pounds.

I tried to call your father and then you, but I had no cell service. I had no choice but to pace and wait for rescue. I have no sense of smell, but I knew that when the small bear charged me, he left his scent on my clothing. I knew the mama could smell it, too, and identify me as the bipedal bear-botherer.

Before long I heard a car approaching and when it came around the bend, I waved it down. The driver came to a stop in the middle of the road and opened the passenger window a couple of inches. "There's a bear down there, her cub charged at me, can you give me a ride?" I blurted. And the woman said, "I don't know you." It was just my luck that at this moment the mama bear had retreated into the woods.

I pleaded with the woman that this was a matter of safety. I was nearly in tears. "I live at the farm right down the road!" "Well, I'll drive along next to you while you walk." This would have left me just as exposed to the vigilant mama bear. I'm a middle-aged broad with the muscle tone of a raw clam and I don't think my appearance is intimidating, especially in yoga pants. Yet this schweinehund wouldn't give me a lift to save me from a Leonardo DiCaprio-in-*The-Revenant* situation.

I didn't have much choice. I couldn't force my way into her car. I told her, "Okay, go, I will find somebody who will help me." I was weak in the knees, tears welling in my eyes, trembling with a confluence of emotions. I was angry and disappointed that she wouldn't help a fellow human. I wasn't asking for a kidney; I was asking to sit in the trunk of her car to get safely home. My house was in the direction she was going anyway! As this Bad

Samaritan drove away, I reflected that if I did get mauled, at least she'd feel extremely guilty when she read my obituary.

For twenty nerve-racking minutes I watched the mama bear walking her beat, perhaps thinking of recipes. Finally, another car came along and this time the driver was willing to give me a lift.

When I got back home and had the ability to sip a mug of tea without shaking, I thought about bravery. I didn't think I'd been brave in facing down the bear cub. I was stuck in the situation; I had no choice but to do my best. The woman who refused to let me in her car—she was a coward. She had a choice to make, and she chose fear.

I can't fully blame her, though. (Although I can blame her partially.) A great number of our choices are fear-based. There is a lot to fear and it's easy to fall prey to the emotion. This has been a nerve-jangling century. It began with the 2000 election, followed by haunting horrors of 9/11, the ensuing wars, terrorism, the loss of servicemen and servicewomen, economic collapse, Ebola, SARS, bird flu, political jackassery, Zika, racial injustice, environmental crisis, a kakistocracy,* and COVID-19. We've had the pants scared off us on numerous occasions, and we're a family that *didn't* take in a savage wild bear and make it wear a doggie Christmas sweater and reindeer antlers.

You and your pals were born in this century and it's all you've known. You really haven't experienced a time when the world was peaceful, just, and healthy. Even our home has not always been a refuge; Hurricane Sandy forced us from it for weeks. It's been a lot, but you've held up well. You deserve a medal for bravery.

* Kakistocracy means "government by the worst people."

You didn't set out to be brave in the face of everything that's been hurled at you. You have it within you, and your father and I have tried to encourage it. It's within everyone to be brave. Courage is not absence of fear, it's acting in the face of fear. Each day brings risks, everything from slipping on a banana peel, to ripping a foghorn fart in chapel, to getting pancaked by a meteor. You don't quiver in your room under the covers, though; you get up and go out in the world. Possibilities for disaster* are also opportunities for bravery. See, this is why I call you Braveheart.

The Real Braveheart

If you've seen the movie, you may be under the impression that Robert the Bruce was a bad guy. Actually, he was a fierce warrior, and it was Robert, not Mel Gibson's William Wallace, who was called Braveheart. In exile because his throne had been usurped, Robert took shelter in a cave. He observed a spider trying to make a web. It launched itself repeatedly into the air but failed to make it. Finally, the determined spider reached its destination. Robert was inspired; he resolved to win back his kingdom and was successful.

It's not clear what killed him, but he didn't die in battle. Some think the rich diet of a king did him in, because his physician had warned him about his excessive consumption of eels. He was so beloved that after his death, his heart was removed from his body. One of his knights had the dried-out heart put in a sort of oversize locket that he wore around his neck and went off to fight the

* Disaster comes from Latin, meaning "bad star." A meteor falling on your head would be a bad star indeed.

Moors in Spain. In a desperate moment, the knight tore off the locket, spiraled it like a football at his opponents, and shouted, "Lead on, brave heart, I'll follow thee!" He did follow Robert's heart, right into the grave. The knight was killed in the battle, but the heart was returned to Scotland.

* * *

Everyone has bravery within them. Every day, people walk around out in the open, even though falling blue ice from an airplane toilet could plummet thirty thousand feet and turn them into a stinky, flattened corpse. We face up to the danger and we can be inspired by the example of Peter Freuchen in his arctic cave, equipped only with a frozen poop knife. As Seneca said, "Sometimes just to live is an act of bravery."

We all have this resource of courage; why don't we celebrate it? We tend to focus more on our negative thoughts, as if somehow our fears and anxieties are more important than kindness and generosity. Our finer qualities like resilience and bravery, these should be our valued virtues. You can become braver by changing your way of thinking. Honor and nurture your courage. Shift your attention from worry to anticipation. Franklin Delano Roosevelt said, "Courage is not the absence of fear, but rather the assessment that something else is more important than fear." You have the power to make that assessment.

You may remember that in middle school you skated with some high school goons at the Stockdale Arena, named for Admiral James Stockdale and his wife, Sybil Stockdale. James Bond Stockdale (his actual middle name) was a heroic Navy pilot who flew nearly two hundred missions in his lifetime. He had studied at Stanford, and a professor gave him a copy of Epictetus's *Enchiridion*, a word that means, roughly, "a manual for living." Stockdale devoted himself to practicing Stoic philosophy and always kept the works of Epictetus near to hand.

In 1965, Stockdale was flying a mission during the Vietnam War when his plane was hit by enemy fire. He had no choice but to bail out. As he drifted to Earth under his parachute, he thought to himself, "I am now leaving the world of technology and entering the world of Epictetus."

During his seven years as a prisoner in the notorious "Hanoi Hilton," he was repeatedly beaten and tortured. Like his mentor Epictetus, his leg was broken. For a two-year stretch, he had to wear leg irons around the clock.

Captain Stockdale was the highest-ranking Naval officer to be captured in the war and was a leader among the other prisoners. He set out a code of conduct, a sort of *Enchiridion* for his fellow POWs. One of the rules was not to cooperate with the propaganda efforts of the North Vietnamese jailers. He was so determined not to let his captors use him for good publicity that he once beat his own face raw so that he could not be shown in public.

The memorized words of Epictetus were his constant companion and guide. In emulation of the great philosopher, he abandoned fear, and also hope. He observed that the prisoners who were optimistic were the ones who didn't make it, the ones who kept hoping they would be released by a certain date, but it never happened. Stockdale later said, "They died of a broken heart. This is a very important lesson. You must never confuse faith that you will prevail in the end—which you can never afford to lose—with the discipline to confront the most brutal facts of your current reality, whatever they might be."

His highest priority was not to give any information to his captors, especially information about his fellow prisoners. He knew he could keep secrets, even under torture, as long as his interrogators didn't know what to ask.

One day a prison guard intercepted a note from Stockdale to another POW. He knew the note would give his torturers leads to pursue, and he knew he'd be tortured for information. He didn't think he would be able to hold back. Other prisoners would be in danger. The night before he was to be interrogated, he managed to break a window and cut his wrists with the jagged glass.

Stockdale was discovered by a guard and the prison doctors saved his life. The American POWs were never tortured again.

He recovered from his near death in isolation. Months later, he was moved back to a section of the prison with other captives. His return was noticed by a fellow prisoner; the sound of Stockdale's distinctive limp tipped him off. He left Stockdale an unsigned note, with the letters printed in rat droppings. On the flimsy scrap of toilet paper was the last verse of the poem "Invictus":

It matters not how strait the gate,
How charged with punishments the scroll,
I am the master of my fate,
*I am the captain of my soul.**

James Stockdale survived his captivity and though he was grievously injured physically, by his own account he came out of prison stronger than he went in. He was awarded the Medal of Honor, the military's highest decoration, and retired with the

* The full text is in the interlude "William Ernest Henley," which follows this chapter.

rank of vice admiral. He wrote a profound book about his experiences called *Thoughts of a Philosophical Fighter Pilot*. Stockdale served as president of the Naval War College and taught philosophy at Stanford. He was even a candidate for vice president of the United States in 1992.

Enduring years in a brutal prison may seem like a hell too daunting to survive for any but the most heroic among us. Fortunately, the vast majority of us will never be tested so severely, but we will be tested. Whatever's coming, it's going to be painful, it will be worrying, it will be gut wrenching, and it's going to leave a mark. This is why it's important to have a philosophy of life.

Stoicism offers wisdom and insight. When you're alone, it offers good company. When you're ambitious, it inspires self-discipline. When you're lazy, it motivates action. When you're fortunate, it reminds you to be grateful and moderate. When you're suffering, it teaches you to dig deep and be resilient. When you are anxious and fearful, it gives you the knowledge that you have the guts to carry on.

Donald Robertson, the best-selling author and noted Stoic philosopher, has a particularly sharp insight: "Worry is a horror story we tell ourselves where we exaggerate the probability, imminence, and severity of a perceived threat and minimize our ability to cope with it." Anxiety and fear want to protect you from harm. In keeping you from engaging the tests you face, they also keep you from the good things in life.

Courage is not a limited resource. In a pinch, you can borrow it. Be inspired by others. Borrow a philosopher's courage, or your mother's. You can borrow courage from the wisdom of Epictetus or the valor of Theodore Roosevelt. Your father or your friends can all lend you courage. They've all been tested. They've all faced huge obstacles. You can borrow courage from your teammates, who are prepared to mix it up with the other guys to protect their goalie. You can repay the loan by letting others borrow from you.

Don't confuse borrowing courage with giving up your belief in your own decisions. You can try to avoid tough challenges by allowing other people to tell you what to do. Coaches, parents, teachers, and friends all have wisdom to share. Do not lose sight of your own wisdom. Marcus Aurelius wrote, "Look well into yourself, there is a source of strength which will always spring up if you will look." Courage is thinking for yourself.

According to actuarial tables, I'm more than halfway through my allotted years, and I'm still growing and learning. My job now is to raise an independent, brave young man of good character. I've learned that to do this I must be an independent, brave woman of good character. It doesn't matter how long you train to be brave, what matters is how you act when you are called to be brave. e. e. cummings, who also rambled the bear-filled forests near our farm, wrote that "it takes courage to grow up and become who you are."

Every day on the outside of a bear is a good day.

With vigor,

Mum

—INTERLUDE—

William Ernest Henley

William Ernest Henley was an English man of letters and a man about town. He was a well-known poet and influential editor and critic of the Victorian era. You always knew when Henley was coming, because he walked with a mono-legged limp.

As a child, he suffered from tuberculosis of the bones. The disease caused him great pain, but young William Ernest mustered his strength to stay cheerful. His brother remarked that he would "hop about the room, laughing loudly and playing with zest to pretend he was beyond the reach of pain."

When William was a teenager, complications from the infection led to the amputation of his left leg below the knee. In his early twenties, doctors recommended that he have the other one lopped off, too, or it was curtains. Henley preferred to keep his remaining lower appendage. He underwent three years of surgeries and hospital stays, and his leg was saved.

Henley met Robert Louis Stevenson while in the hospital and the two became fast friends. When the young poet was up and about again, Stevenson was struck by his powerful upper body and limping gait. Stevenson gave these traits to one of his most famous literary creations, the pirate Long John Silver, whose arrival is announced by the tapping of his wooden leg.

While Henley was undergoing his three-year course of surgeries, he began work on his most famous poem: "Invictus." The verses inspired not only his Victorian contemporaries, but also Nelson Mandela during his long imprisonment. Winston Churchill referred to it in a speech to parliament during the darkest days of World War II. US Congressman John Lewis learned it as a teenager, and it invigorated him throughout his life.

This is the full poem:

Out of the night that covers me,
Black as the pit from pole to pole,
I thank whatever gods may be
For my unconquerable soul.

In the fell clutch of circumstance
I have not winced nor cried aloud.
Under the bludgeonings of chance
My head is bloody, but unbowed.

Beyond this place of wrath and tears
Looms but the Horror of the shade,
And yet the menace of the years
Finds and shall find me unafraid.

It matters not how strait the gate,
How charged with punishments the scroll,
I am the master of my fate,
I am the captain of my soul.

7

DONKEYS AND WEASELS

Dear Smilin' Jack,

When a baby is born to Navajo parents, the starter's pistol goes off for an intense competition among friends of the family. They all want to be the one to provoke the infant's first laugh. Baby's first chuckle is a momentous occasion. The Navajo believe that newborns are still living partially in the spiritual world. The first laugh is a sign that the baby is leaving the spirit world behind and fully committing to life in the physical world with his family.

Some Navajo believe that the baby will take on the personality of the person who provoked that initial giggle. I imagine that friends of the family hang around day and night, looking for an opportunity to tickle the baby or make funny faces or tell dad jokes. The person lucky enough to make junior crack up must throw a party to celebrate the occasion, called A'wee Chi'deedloh. In addition to a meal, the jokester provides gifts of salt and sweets to teach the baby to be generous.

This is not a tradition in our Irish Greek family, but it is a beautiful one. Our friends rejoiced with us when the time came that you laughed and the light really shone in your eyes and we were finally sure you were human and not a jelly-necked larval alien. None of them threw a party, though.

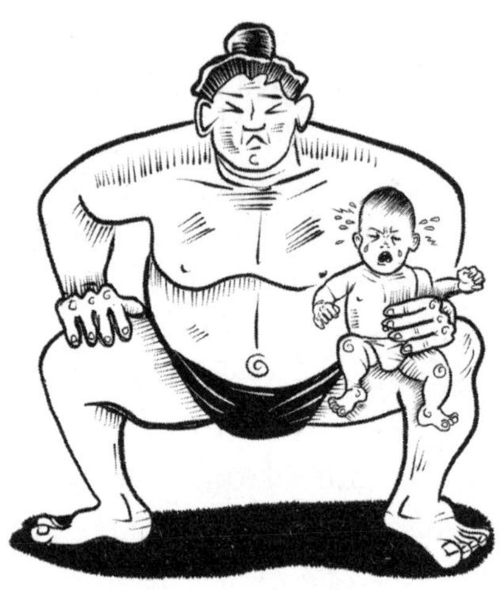

No Sumo, No Cry

In Japan, the four-hundred-year-old tradition of Nakizumo brings roly-poly, apple-cheeked beings, with their bare bottoms clad only in diapers, together with babies. Weighty, man-bunned sumo wrestlers pair off, each holding an infant, and compete to see who can make their kid cry. Usually it's the loser who cries, but at this festival, it's the winner who's in tears. If both babies cry, the winner is the loudest bawler. Parents pay fifteen thousand yen to enter their tots, or about $135, and it is so popular that you must win a lottery to get in. The folk belief is that crying wards off demons, so the wailing child will grow up healthy. Keep this in mind the next time I threaten to give you something to cry about.

Another moment for celebration in a baby's life is when he takes his first steps. Your first steps were momentous, because we were hosting a Super Bowl party and it was the year of the "wardrobe malfunction," when Justin Timberlake revealed one of Janet Jackson's funbags. While we were riveted by the half-time spectacle, you stood up and staggered to the chip bowl.

There is an old Bulgarian tradition called Proshtapulnik, which is a celebration thrown to honor a baby's first steps—not the wobbly, drunken sailor stagger where a baby's gigantic head clocks back and forth like a metronome, but the first real, confident strut between point A and point B. The belief is that a Proshtapulnik party celebrating the first walk without wiping out will ensure that the child won't stumble in life, nor will there be roadblocks to hold the baby back. Bulgarians often joke that when someone trips and does a face plant, it is because their parents didn't host a Proshtapulnik party for them.

If you could mash up the Navajo A'wee Chi'deedloh and the Bulgarian Proshtapulnik party, we would have celebrated it one sunny morning on vacation at the lake. We were with a big group of friends and one couple had brought their baby along. During a breakfast feast out on the patio, little Edgar pulled himself up on a chair, let go, and took his first few tentative paces. Everyone cheered for Edgar's unsteady steps, and Bill Murray, who was eating a banana, very casually tossed the peel in front of the tyke. We cracked up, and luckily Edgar did not crack his skull. In the museum of memories I carry in my head, this is like Rodin's *Thinker*. It still makes me laugh.

The average adult laughs seventeen times a day, and the average child laughs three hundred times a day. Laughter brings in big gusts of oxygen and stimulates the release of endorphins, a neurotransmitter that makes us feel good. It's a physical sensation as well as an emotional experience.

Laughing isn't just a reaction to a stimulus, like a tickle or the sight of a baby slipping on a banana peel. It is a form of communication, a way of showing that you understand and like the person who made you laugh. Laughing together is a bonding experience. You are thirty times more likely to laugh when talking to your friends.

Sober Sue

In the early 1900s, the Paradise Roof Garden theater featured a performer billed as "Sober Sue," the girl who never laughed. The producers offered one hundred dollars to the person who could make Sue crack a smile and one thousand dollars for a belly laugh. Audience members told their funniest jokes, professional comedians delivered their knee-slapping best, but she never so much as smirked, and no one ever won the prize. Turns out, there was nothing wrong with Sue's sense of humor; she had Moebius syndrome, a condition affecting the cranial nerves, which causes an unmoving, mask-like expression. Sober Sue got twenty dollars a week for sitting in a chair and not laughing, which was a pretty good wage at the time. No pictures of her survive, but her name lives on among theater folk as a slang term for a tough, unsmiling audience. Theater reviews used to say of comedies that they were so funny, they could even make Sober Sue laugh.

Eminent scientist Dr. Robin Dunbar calls laughter "grooming from a distance." Just as a troop of chimps builds social bonds by picking through each other's fur for lice, you and your knucklehead buddies strengthen your friendship when you crack up over episodes of *Family Guy*. Laughter greases the wheels of friendship.

Friends make us laugh, and it's said that laughter is the best medicine; perhaps that's why Ecclesiastes 6:16 tells us that "a faithful friend is the medicine of life." No doctor can write a prescription for friendship or surgically implant the power of companionship. The love and laughs you share with friends are a natural performance-enhancing supplement.

You are influenced the most by the five people you spend the most time with. I've been best friends with the same group since middle school. There are four of us: Lori, Lynn, Greg, and me. (I know that's only three friends, but you and your father round out my top five). We all went to high school together. Lori and I went to the same college, and we then roomed together with Lynn after graduation. Greg lived across the street. Lori lives in the same building we do now, and Lynn and Greg are across the street from each other. We've stayed close.

Other people have tried to join the circle of "inside friends," but I am adamant. The four of us cannot be augmented. Anyone else will have to remain an outside friend—sorry, Mariella, and regrets, Gianna; you are wonderful, but you cannot come inside.

Ralph Waldo Emerson wrote that "it is one of the blessings of old friends that you can afford to be stupid with them." You've seen me with Greg, Lynn, and Lori, and you know that's true. My inside friends are wiseasses and jokers. Laughter cements our friendship. One Christmas we were all broke and set a five-dollar limit on gifts. The most memorable present that year was from Lynn, who went to Chinatown and bought us each a chicken foot for the low price of twenty-five cents per.

That night we went out dancing and hid the chicken feet in our sleeves to scare away unwanted attention.

Lori started her career working for an advertising firm but decided to strike out on her own. She needed to land a big client, and pursued one guy relentlessly, but he wouldn't reply to her calls. Then she discovered that the big cheese was in the hospital. He'd been stricken by an infection that caused his testes to swell up to the size of cantaloupes and was not up to doing any business.*

Lori was undaunted. She made a circus attraction-like poster that read, "SEE THE MAN WITH THE WORLD'S BIGGEST BALLS—50 CENTS TO LOOK—ONE DOLLAR TO TOUCH—FIVE DOLLARS TO POKE THEM AS HARD AS YOU CAN." She sent him the poster tucked into a flower arrangement, and instead of being outraged, he laughed (gingerly, I suppose). She got the job. Lori went on to win a Cannes Lion, the highest award in advertising.

When we were just out of college, Greg would cut our hair and hand-tailor our clothes so we looked fashionable enough to get into New York nightclubs. He called us "bait"—three bright young things were enough to get him admitted to a club, too. We couldn't always afford the cover charges, so we came up with cockamamie schemes to get in free. One night Greg came home with an enormous trench coat for me to wear. I climbed up on his shoulders and buttoned the coat on. Stacked up like this we were eight feet tall. When we got to the doorman, I chirped, "Admission for one, please." The doorman cracked up and said, "Fine, but you have to stay that way all night."

* In pagan Rome, they had no bibles to use when making a solemn oath. Instead, men would grab their own family jewels and swear on their testes, which is where we get the word "testify."

Seneca advised us to "associate with those who will make a better man of you." We have lived up to this maxim. I beam with pride when I think of all three of my "inside friends" and their great successes. It's been a wild ride cheering them on. "Mudita" is a Sanskrit word that describes the joy you feel in the success and joy of others. I feel this intensely about Lynn, Greg, and Lori.

I would take a bullet for my closest friends. I would donate a kidney if they needed it. I have trusted them to bob my hair. They challenge and inspire me. I view them as fearless and that spurs me to be fearless. I wouldn't have accomplished what I have without them. I'm doing what I love because of them. I'm fortunate to be able to speak to the world through books, and I might not be here if they hadn't goaded me into sending an audition tape to MTV when I was still a recreational therapist.

The classical Greeks valued friendship more highly than marriage. Most marriages were arranged. Friendships were chosen and were a most revered relationship. Plato placed such a high value on intense, non-sexual relationships that the term "platonic friendship" describes just this kind of fellowship.*

Heroic friendship was a term that described a deep intellectual and emotional bond. In ancient times, this connection often existed between warriors who were bound to fight side by side and protect each other. I'm not a soldier and neither are you, but I have these deep bonds with my inside friends, and I am a better person for it. The book of Proverbs tells us that "as iron sharpens iron, so a man sharpens the countenance of his friend." Lori, Lynn, and Greg have honed me razor-sharp.

---

* I've sometimes wondered what Plato called *his* non-sexual relationships. "Friend-zoned"? "Friends without benefits"? "Me-atonic"?

There is a random, magical quality about friendship. Of the eight billion humans who are on this big rock, revolving around an even bigger ball of fire, you pick a few to be your friends. Then you cheer for each other, you love each other, you laugh together, and when they stop breathing, water comes out of your eyes.

Surround yourself with supportive people. You will lift and inspire each other and buck each other up when you've had setbacks. Friendship encourages individual achievements as well as collective success. Creating and sustaining friendships is a big part of living a good life. As Epicurus, the founder of the Epicurean school of philosophy, wrote, "Of all the means to ensure happiness throughout the whole life, by far, the most important is the presence of friends."

Every summer, we travel to Toronto for your hockey camp. We stay at a hotel out in the suburbs, several cuts below my usual standard, which isn't that high to begin with. On our first visit, we found the lobby filled with people dressed in what looked like college mascot costumes. One woman had wings so large I could barely edge around her. I asked the bemused desk clerk what was going on, and he informed me that the hotel was hosting the largest furry convention in North America. He explained that furries are people who enjoy dressing up in enormous plush outfits.

You were at the rink all day, so I spent some time among the furries. When you got back that night, I told you what I had done, and you were scandalized. "You could have been attacked and roofied!" you scolded me. I didn't know you had formed such strongly negative impressions about furries at such a tender age.

Being among these costumed comrades was strange for me, but when they took their oversized furry heads off, I could see their faces were filled with love and camaraderie. These were people with a particular hobby that made them outsiders to me, but here they were with their people. They had found their circle of inside friends.*

When you were younger, you chose hockey over play dates and birthday parties. You had hockey bros, but you were essentially a lone wolf. I was a little worried for you because friendship is deeply important. You're now in high school and you have started to make those connections—not with furries, although I wouldn't judge.

Friendships will be some of the longest relationships of your life, yet we don't value them as highly as marriage, domestic partnership, or parenthood. There are no ceremonies like marriage to start it, no divorce to end it; it's all up to you to keep it alive. The beauty of friendship is that it is voluntary.

Friendship is foundational to our existence. Philosophers have spilled barrels of ink on it. Aristotle insisted that "no one would choose to live without friendship." Bill Murray, another noted philosopher, had this to say: "Friendship is weird. You just pick a human you've met and you're like 'Yup, I like this one,' and you just do stuff with them." Friendship is a joyride you take together. You can fall in friendship with a friend as profoundly as you can fall in love with a lover.

There are different levels of friendship that aren't easily expressed by one word. The English language has a poverty of words for friendship, just as it does for love. (Our mother tongue is not so good with relationships, I guess.) There is only one word to describe the person you just met, your buddy from high

* As for me, I found a gently used, slightly soiled chipmunk costume for just sixty Canadian dollars.

school twenty years ago, and the fella in the next cubicle who cheers for the same team you do. I would say there are four levels of friendship:

1. Acquaintance. What's your name again?
2. Pal. If you were a chimp, they'd groom you.
3. Three a.m. bro. The guy who bails you out of the pokey.
4. Best man.

You tend to stockpile the friends you make in early adulthood. Social research suggests that your popularity peaks at age twenty-three. These friends are the seeds for your social garden. As you get older, making friends becomes trickier. You settle into a unit. That unit may be a wide circle of acquaintances, a small coterie of pals, your immediate family, or just your own hermit self.

Ornamental Hermits

Wealthy eighteenth-century Englishmen may have had grand homes and extensive manicured grounds, but for many, something was missing. These restless aristocrats created rocky grottoes in which a hermit could reside, providing the finishing touch to their estates. Authentic hermits were few and far between, though, and soon there was a market in paid hermits. Gentlemen advertised for their services, and would-be "ornamental hermits" placed their own ads seeking employment. The most prized hermits were old men with long, gray beards, and they were not allowed to cut their hair or nails. Guests at country estates were invited to come gawk at the faux holy men in their artificial caves. Some grotto residents recited poetry, while others were required to remain mute. The hermits received room and board, but no payday until the end of their years-long employment.

* * *

Your friend group will tend to shrink as you ratchet up in years. The only new people you meet may be work acquaintances. Old friends will fall away. Some will move to Antarctica; others will marry heinous shrews or blowhard bores. You'll devote more of your time to fewer friends. Forty-five percent of adults say it's hard to make new friends, and 42 percent said shyness was a problem for them. The average American adult hasn't made a new friend in five years.

With your circle in danger of shrinking, you may feel you have to hold on to the friends you have at all costs. They are your bros. I used to prize loyalty to friends as an iron-clad part of my personality and one of the virtues I honored most highly.

I learned I was mistaken. You don't have to be loyal to someone who doesn't bring out your best, challenge you, make you smarter, encourage you to take risks, and back you up if you fail. I have been blessed with so many great friends who have those traits, and I assumed all of my friends did. It was yet another late-in-life epiphany that loyalty has limits.

Jack, there are two types of friends: jackasses and weasels. Jackasses, contrary to the popular image of ornery, stubborn beasts, are deeply loyal and will enrich your life and make you a better human. Weasels are draining and a heavy lift.

Weasels are sneaky beasts that eat chickens and can suck out the insides of an egg without breaking the shell. They kill and eat half their weight every day and will kill even when they're stuffed to the gills. When they have another animal cornered, they do a mesmerizing dance to confuse and distract their prey before going for the jugular. The Greeks thought weasels were unhappy brides transformed into an animal. Native Americans thought they were a bad omen.

A group of weasels is called a sneak, or a confusion. This describes human weasels well, although they most often operate alone—it's every man for himself when you're a weasel. They are draining, thieving. They don't take responsibility for their lousy lives.

When one friend in particular began to suffer a string of bad breaks, I stood by him. When he began to act like a weasel, I stayed his friend. I believed I was being compassionate; I was suffering along with him. I was motivated by another close pal who shared my simple belief that you never turn your back on a friend, even if you don't like him anymore. Turned out it wasn't that simple.

I watched this guy cheat and fail over and over. He made repeated bad decisions and took no responsibility for them. He designed and participated in his descent into the weasel den. Every lapse of character was an opportunity to plead for more help from someone else, especially his dwindling circle of friends.

As his life fell apart, I stayed in contact, believing that my spiritual backbone made me tough enough to deal with his negativity and that it would show weakness of character to abandon him. I watched him borrow money he would never repay. I saw him stiff people on his bills. I watched him destroy his own home in the process of carrying out another get-rich-quick fantasy. All the while I imagined that my friendship could lend him the courage to get out of his spiral. I didn't want to leave him friendless.

Finally, my friend Megan suggested to me that when someone suffers a seemingly endless series of misfortunes, don't make an automatic calculation that he is a noble victim of fate and bad juju. All of these difficulties—broken relationships, unemployment, outright fraud to stave off the bill collectors—were not the result of colossal bad luck. Sticking by him made me complicit in his delusion that he had no responsibility for his situation. He rejected the opportunities to get on track or even get a job because it demanded responsibility on his end. I was infantilizing a guy who I once looked up to, buying into his view of himself as a helpless victim. As my wise pal Megan noted, "There is nothing more boring or less sexy than someone claiming victimhood."

The fact that he'd lost all of his friends should have been a sign. Socrates warned that good people are friends with good people, but bad people have no friends.

I had to keep this friend compartmentalized. I was embarrassed to have him around. I didn't want him around you. I was feeding this weasel and he was trying to suck life out of me. So, finally, I decided to drop him as a friend.

Loyalty is a bond that is fair and honest. It's not a one-way street. Friendship is reciprocal. In the *Nicomachean Ethics*, Aristotle writes, "Friends are people who must be mutually recognized as bearing goodwill and wishing well to each other." Loyalty is not a virtue when it comes with an expense. The expense could be a loss of respect from others. The expense could be an actual expense when they start weaseling money off you.

When I drive by his foreclosed house, my disgust still bubbles up, but I remind myself to be grateful that I don't have a victim mentality and am not a thief. When I feel anger about his lies, I turn it into something positive. Every time I let myself indulge in revenge theater, I make a donation to the food bank. I turn my loathing and disappointment into something better for all. As Epictetus said, "Never be so tied to former friends that you are pulled down to their level."

If you keep a friend away from people you love, if you wouldn't want your mom or your cousin to have that person as a friend, dump him. You are not bound by childish rules of friendship that make you responsible for supporting a bum. Don't beat yourself up over evicting a creepy weasel from your life. You deserve a better friend. Epictetus admonished us, "The key is to keep company only with people who uplift you, whose purpose calls forth your best." Part of the responsibility of being of good character is to protect yourself from weasels and all kinds of smelly rodents.

Life is too short for weasels. They are going to be all around you. The only upside we can take from weasels and difficult people is to use them as examples of how we will not behave. Marcus Aurelius noted that "the best revenge is to not be like your enemy." (Enemy is a strong word, but remember, the Emperor Philosopher King led armies and fended off assassins.)

You might work for a weasel. You might be governed by one. You might be seated next to a weasel who takes off their shoes on an airplane.* Your ability to deal with these weasels is

* My friend Matt told me that he was on a long-haul international flight, and the old man next to him took off his shoes. Matt said that the smell was a slap in the face. The stink took human form and chased him about the cabin. The stewardess knew exactly what to do and they gave the geezer two bags of coffee beans. They asked the man to kindly place his corn-chip-toenailed, bunioned feet into the bags for the rest of the flight. Matt said that the guy didn't seem to think it was an odd request, and he parked his feet in the coffee bags for the entirety of the nine-hour trip. Please don't drink coffee on airplanes.

limited. You can't control them; you can only control how you react to them.

Part of being a good friend is being a good friend to yourself. Don't allow a weasel to remain in your circle of friends. Weed your social garden and pull them out by the roots.

If you need any more reason to keep weasels out of your life, consider this: Like skunks, weasels brew up a foul substance in glands on their rear end. When cornered, they can fire stink bombs out their butts, right into your damn face.

Jack, you've got a nose for weasels. I had another friend who was trending in a sketchy direction and one day you piped up and said, "I don't want him around." Trust your instincts. If you think you're dealing with a weasel in friend's clothing, banish him.

Your true friends will have the characteristics of the beloved jackasses on our farm, Jake and Mason. They are affectionate, intelligent, and good listeners. They have excellent memories; I always bring them extra carrots, which is why they get so annoyed when you bring them a regular ration. They're herd animals and like hanging out with us as much as we like hanging out with them.

Donkeys are gentle and react positively to human affection. They have a soothing effect on high-strung racehorses, and on high-strung humans, too. Donkeys are such calm, emotionally intelligent quadrupeds, they are used as assistive therapy animals in hospices. They poke their noses through bedroom windows and residents stroke their soft, fuzzy muzzles.

Jackasses form close bonds. They maintain and strengthen those bonds by grooming, just as chimpanzees do. They are protective and guard our cattle from coyotes and wolves, as well as weasels.*

Jackasses are philosophical. They are natural Stoics; they take life as it comes and don't complain. They are the symbol of the Democratic party, and though I don't know Jake and Mason's exact politics, I suspect they are utilitarians and believe in the greater good.

Our jackasses love to laugh. We are their friends, and we laugh with them. We also laugh at their comical ears and buck teeth. They don't mind. Being around them is like watching an episode of *Hee Haw*, only funny. How can you not flash a radiant smile when looking at a donkey?

Jake and Mason are brothers and bosom friends, but they will scrap from time to time. They chase each other around the pasture, nipping at each other's necks. They play tug of war with branches and can get their dander up. You're going to have disagreements with your friends, too, and you have to know how to patch things up.

If you lived in Santo Tomás, Peru, you would fix up a squabble at the festival of Takanakuy. This means "to hit each other" in the Quechua language. Every year on Christmas Day, anyone with a grudge squares off with their opponent. The two fight until one asks for mercy. All are welcome to participate: men, women, children, even donkeys or llamas for all I know. After the fight, the two brawlers hug, differences are set aside, and friendship is restored. It all happens on Jesus's birthday.

* I was cleaning up after a late-night party one morning, and I picked up an empty cardboard case of beer. At least I thought it was empty, until a small weasel jumped out and did that dance where it tried to hypnotize me. It didn't work, as far as I know, but I quit smoking and I did lose ten pounds.

Takanakuy is kind of like a hockey fight. At the end of the game, you guys all shake hands and skate off.

A tradition I prefer takes place in Glencoe, Scotland. When two friends get in a dispute, they abide by an ancient ritual to settle their differences. The two row out to a small island in Loch Leven with a supply of cheese, oatcakes, and whiskey. The parties remain on the Island of Discussion until they have hashed out a solution.

If the whiskey isn't finished at that point, I'm guessing they hang out until it is. For myself, I prefer to have a drop with my friends to smooth any problems over before they start.

Marcus Aurelius's *Meditations* contains a series of thank-yous to the people who helped make him the man he is. I'd like to do the same because friends make us more than who we are alone. Friends raise you up, and you can borrow their strengths and ride on their coattails.

Peg thinks there's always a solution to any hitch. She has taught me to be unconquerable, that every problem can be figured out. I strive to be the person Peg thinks I could be.

Debi is fearless. I once went along to visit her grandma in Queens. When we came out of the building, some toughs were sprawled all over her car. I'm a chicken. I was scared. Debi just said, briskly, "All right boys, it's time to go." They slouched off. Seeing her in action stiffened my own spine, just a little.

George taught me the value of true loyalty, great storytelling, and expertise in pranks.

Bill is a natural Stoic, taking life as it comes and enjoying it at every turn.

Andrew taught me about kindness and vigor and is a virtuoso in turning obstacles into opportunity.

For Aristotle, friendship was a necessary part of eudaimonia, meaning a happy, flourishing life. I get a lot of different things from my friends, but as W. H. Auden said, "Among those who I like or admire, I can find no common denominator, but among those whom I love: all of them make me laugh."

A friend is one of the best things you can have and one of the best things you can be.

Let's crowd the world with this spirit,

Mum

8

UNCLE GOLDEN TOE

Dear Jack,

Your great-great-uncle Stephen Capestro was the brother of the only grandfather I knew, our beloved step-grandfather, John Baptiste Capestro. Uncle Steve lived a long and eventful life. He was a football star at Rutgers University, nicknamed Golden Toe because he was such a good kicker.* His father, who had been born in Italy, would cheer him on: "Stefano, va, va!" ("Go, Stephen, go!")

When the United States entered World War II, Uncle Steve was drafted into the army. He was recruited into the Office of Strategic Services (OSS), the precursor to the Central Intelligence Agency (CIA), which was the department responsible for spying and sabotage. After intense training, including as a paratrooper, he was sent to North Africa. His commanding officer was Jack Hemingway, son of Ernest.

---

* Appendages of precious metal run in both sides of your family. Your great-grandfather on your father's side owned the Royal typewriter company, and he was commissioned by Ian Fleming to make a gold typewriter. It was on this gilded machine that Fleming composed the James Bond novel *Goldfinger*.

One of the missions of the OSS was to place camouflaged explosives where they would do the most damage to the enemy. In Europe, bombs were disguised as lumps of coal and logs, but in North Africa, these items were not lying around in abundance and would have provoked suspicion. Harvard anthropologist and OSS officer Carleton Coon came up with the idea of disguising bombs as poop. He sent samples of mule and camel droppings to London for analysis. The scientists observed that the desert dung was smaller than English road apples and had a brown color with hints of green. Thus educated, Uncle Steve and his OSS comrades could get down to the business of blowing shit up.

Aunt Jemima

THE OSS DIDN'T just hide bombs in what came out of the end of the digestive tract, they disguised explosives as what went into the beginning. To the American intelligence service, "Aunt Jemima" was not a spy but the code name for an explosive baking powder. The flaming flour was invented by George Bogdan Kistiakowsky, a chemist turned soldier who later worked on the atomic bomb. "Aunt Jemima" was designed and packaged to look and act like flour. It could even be baked into muffins and consumed without exploding. (But I bet it blew up the toilet.) To make explosive flapjacks or doughnuts for a sabotage mission, guerillas added an accelerant and a small detonator to make a delicious dessert bombe.

Uncle Golden Toe was a great spy. No one in our family even knew he was a secret agent until my brother uncovered an oral history in which he talked about his experiences. He broke his back in a truck accident while serving, but we never knew it was while doing clandestine duty.

Virginia Hall also served in the OSS. Hall was the most highly decorated female civilian during World War II. Her road to skulduggery did not run as smoothly as Uncle Golden Toe's.

Virginia came from an upper-crust background but was a tomboy who rebelled against the straitjacket of her class. Hall described herself as capricious and cantankerous. Her high school classmates voted her "Most Original," which was not a compliment. She once went to school wearing a bracelet made of live snakes. Virginia was apparently an avid if incautious hunter; while hunting birds in Turkey, she shot herself in the foot. Gangrene spread up her leg and the injured limb had to be amputated. She was fitted with a wooden leg, which she called "Cuthbert."*

Your body is 50 percent legs, and Hall lost 50 percent of that. Rather than grieving at her long, painful recovery and one-legged existence, she felt that shooting herself in the leg had given her a second shot at life, and she wasn't going to throw it away. Her injury reignited her resilience and commitment to continue her life of vigor and duty to her country.

* I like to think that if Virginia Hall had ever been on a mission with Uncle Golden Toe, he would have called her . . . Wooden Toe.

Hall worked in the diplomatic corps as a secretary but wanted to be a full-fledged foreign service officer. She applied multiple times but was refused on the grounds of an obscure rule that prohibited anyone with a disability from serving. This decision was appealed to President Franklin Delano Roosevelt, whose bout with polio had left him in a wheelchair, but to no avail.

When World War II broke out, she journeyed to France and served as an ambulance driver. A chance meeting with an English spy led to Hall joining the Special Operations Executive (SOE), the British version of the OSS. Hall served as an undercover agent in Vichy, France, for two years. The Gestapo gave her the nickname "Artemis"* and considered her the most dangerous Allied spy.

When things got too precarious in France, Hall hot-footed it to Spain over the treacherous, snowy mountain passes of the Pyrenees in the dead of winter, dragging Cuthbert along. She made her way back to London, where the SOE refused to send her back to France because they believed she was now too well known. She applied to the OSS instead, which ordered her to organize and support armed French resistance to the Nazis.

Hall knew she would need better cover this time around if she were to avoid capture and execution. A makeup artist taught her to draw wrinkles on her face. A dentist ground down her gleaming, healthy white American teeth to gray little nubs. She learned to walk with an old woman's shuffle to disguise her limp. The vibrant thirty-six-year-old Baltimore socialite transformed herself into an old French peasant.

* Artemis was the Greek goddess of hunting, wild nature, and chastity and was the patron of young women.

Virginia Hall was one of America's most important spies (outside our family members). President Truman awarded the Distinguished Service Cross to her, the only female civilian to receive one in World War II. France bestowed upon her the Croix de Guerre, and she was made an honorary member of the Order of the British Empire.

Before the war, Virginia Hall couldn't get the job of her dreams. Middle-aged women can feel invisible. The male bureaucrats in the State Department couldn't see her qualities. She was undeterred, and she forged a new path on one leg and made her mark—ironically, in a job for which she had to hide her identity. Hall always had to navigate past obstacles, and during the war was respected more by her enemies than her allies.

In life, some people push the envelope, some lick it. It's up to you to choose. Virginia Hall was a pusher, not a licker.

When she was faced with something that blocked her way forward, she went around it, blew it up, or reinvented herself. We often think of young people as the ones who remake themselves with every new trend or reading of *The Catcher in the Rye*. Reinvention isn't just for young people, though. Middle-aged women are the greatest phoenixes to arise on our planet. Sometimes we rise because our worth has been undervalued. Sometimes it's because we have raised children, and when the time comes to let them fly, we are then free to channel our talents in a new direction. Midlife crisis has a negative connotation, but really, it's a midlife opportunity. Obstacles are a chance to shake up the ossified view of who you are.

Reinvention is reinvigorating later in life. We have more experience. Eighty percent of middle-aged women feel younger than they are, and the same number feel underestimated. Virginia Hall was misjudged too.

I think middle-aged moms would actually make great spies. We are excellent at working hard on a tight schedule, managing multiple tasks, and keeping a friendly covering smile when talking to that nag Karen on the PTA. Certainly we are good at baking and are able to whip up some explosive popovers with "Aunt Jemima."

Take inspiration from middle-aged women, no matter your age or gender. Your life will have obstacles between you and where you want to go. I fervently hope these will not include shooting your leg off, but your path will not always run smooth. Marcus Aurelius wrote, "The impediment to action advances action. What stands in the way becomes the way." Or as the prodigious modern Stoic Ryan Holiday titled his excellent book, *The Obstacle Is the Way*.

The biggest obstacle we face is that we don't think we'll face obstacles. My dad, an ex-cop, would often remind us that the problem is that we don't expect problems. "If you anticipate the coming of troubles, you can take away some of their power when they arrive," cautioned Socrates, who I'm thinking may have had a lot of obstacles to deal with as he was handed his cup of hemlock.

Early on in the pandemic, I checked in to see how you were coping. You noted that some kids will sink and some will swim. It is a choice, and you swam like Gertrude Ederle* toward your goals. You didn't just float with the tide, despite the tempest that was raging. The young philosophical troublemaker Hunter S. Thompson was asked for life advice by a friend, and

* Teenager Gertude Ederle was the first woman to swim across the English Channel. She was lauded as "America's Best Girl" by President Calvin Coolidge. Songs were written in her honor, and she received a torrent of wedding proposals by mail. She won gold at the 1924 Olympics and set a world record in the process.

Thompson responded, "Who is the happier man, he who has braved the storm of life and lived or he who has stayed securely on shore and merely existed?"

The pandemic had been a stormy time. Schools around the world switched to online learning as a result of the global health crisis. As your challenges grew, you grew into a different young man. You turned half of our garage into a gym and, with your dad, installed artificial ice in the other half. Your plan was to outwork everybody. You turned the obstacles of a canceled hockey season into an opportunity to create a season of training. You kept your eye on the puck, had fun, and had your best academic semester.

A Stoic doesn't give up, doesn't accept lower standards, and never expects less of themselves. Uncle Golden Toe got the OSS medal for living these values. I know your ancestors would be proud of you for doing the same.

It doesn't escape me that I am writing a letter to you about overcoming obstacles and reaching your goals, and your job as a goaltender is to be an obstacle to other people's goals.

Your Stoic Mum

9

SMALL CARROTS

Dear Jack,

You may think of classical philosophers as dead-boring gasbags who spent all day pondering the nature of existence and wrestling with titanic moral questions. You imagine modern philosophers sitting in cafes, sipping espresso, and dropping Gauloise ash on their black turtlenecks, projecting an air of existential ennui and shifting uncomfortably because of the sticks up their butts. In truth, philosophers are a subversive and brilliant collection of crackpots.

Diogenes the Cynic turned his back on his wealthy banker father. He slept in an enormous wine jar in the center of ancient Athens as the ultimate expression of his commitment to living humbly.

The word "cynic," or "kynikos," is the Greek word for dog. The term was used as an insult, but Diogenes embraced it, saying, "I fawn on those who give me anything, I yelp at those who refuse, and I set my teeth in rascals." He believed that humans could learn much from dogs and should emulate the simplicity of their existence. Like a dog, he relieved himself in public, and in ancient Athens, there were no pooper scooper laws. Good thing he couldn't lick his balls like our puppy, Fredo. He believed the purpose of existence was to live a life of virtue, but he was caught spanking the monkey in public. Plato referred to him as "Socrates gone mad."

Pythagoras was an eccentric genius mathematician who coined the word "philosophy," meaning "love of wisdom." He also had some bonkers beliefs that included not eating beans, possibly because he thought that the excessive wind they caused stole the very breath of life. Or possibly because he believed that beans held the reincarnated souls of humans, and that "eating fava beans and gnawing on the heads of one's parents are one and the same."*

When Pythagoras snubbed a wealthy young man who demanded a meeting, the lout whipped up a mob to attack the philosopher. The rabble burned down his house and chased the wise man until he came up against a bean field. Not wanting to trample the musical fruit, Pythagoras stopped his flight and the mob caught up. He was stabbed to death, but his beloved beans were unharmed.

Jeremy Bentham was an English philosopher and Britain's answer to Aristotle. He was a radical thinker, a social reformer with a heart as big as his head, and an eccentric in the grandest tradition of English eccentrics.†

* I guess when Hannibal Lecter ate someone's liver with fava beans, he was committing double cannibalism. These healthy legumes are loaded with vitamins, minerals, fiber, protein, and a legacy of savagery.

† "Eccentric" comes originally from the Greek "ek kentron," meaning "off center." Today it means someone who's got a screw or two loose.

Like Aristotle, he did lots of thinking on long morning walks. Unlike Aristotle, he was accompanied on his peripatetic perambulations by a walking stick he named Dapple.

Back at home, Bentham poured himself a warming cup from a "sacred teapot" he called Dickey. His elderly cat, Reverend Sir Doctor Langbourne, sat on his lap as he worked. At night, his pet pig curled up in bed and kept him cozy. His motto was, "Create all the happiness you are able to create; remove all the misery you are able to remove. Every day will allow you, will invite you to add something to the pleasure of others, or to diminish something of their pains." His life was filled with the love of his pets and of all humanity.

The Cat Piano

Athanasius Kircher was a seventeenth-century Jesuit priest and scholar. The versatile vicar studied volcanoes, Egyptian hieroglyphs, and the plague, but I prefer to remember him for an invention that would have horrified Jeremy Bentham: the cat piano. A series of cats whose voices ranged from low purr, to middle meow, to high yowl would be arranged in a line of cages. Pressing a key on the "katzenklavier" would send a poke into a cat's tail and produce a symphony of feline outrage. Kircher invented this harpsichord of horror to "raise the spirits of an Italian prince burdened by the cares of his position." There is no evidence that the cat piano was ever built, or any record of what happened to the spirits of the Italian prince.

As the Industrial Revolution gathered steam, Bentham raised his voice against the exploitation of children and the most vulnerable. He campaigned for prison reform and proposed the decriminalization of homosexuality. Equal rights for women was one of his most firmly held beliefs. He opposed cruelty of any kind and was a pioneer advocate for animal welfare. He was a fountain of human kindness and progressive ideas.

Bentham was the founder of modern utilitarianism. His highest principle was that "it is the greatest happiness of the greatest number that is the measure of right and wrong." This isn't necessarily a Stoic principle, but it is an idea I like to keep in mind when weighing whether or not to play our cat piano.

He was a man of great conviction in life and in death. In accordance with his last wishes, when he died, his friends were invited to the dissection of his corpus. Once the organs had been removed, his body was reassembled, dressed in his clothes, and placed in a glass cabinet.

Bentham believed no one should profit from death, except society. He wanted everyone to be displayed after their death because even a corpse could contribute to the common good. For Bentham, the most important thing you can leave behind is a legacy, even if it is a bit eccentric.

His intent was to have his mummified head placed atop the "auto-icon," as he called his preserved, stuffed body. The blue glass eyes used for the purpose were a pair that he had carried in his pocket during life. The desiccated noggin proved too grotesque, though, so a wax head was made instead (just as grotesque, if you ask me). The actual head was hidden away . . . at the feet of the Bentham mummy, in plain view.* His taxidermied body wound up on display at University College London, where his remains remain today.

Bentham led an unusual life and has led an even more unusual afterlife. We often wish for the dead to "rest in peace," but sadly that is not what happened to dead Jeremy. He rests in pieces. His decapitated head became a prize for thieves, usually drunk undergraduates. It has become a tradition for Jeremy's head to be kidnapped by a rival college, and in one case, the missing cranium was discovered in a train station storage locker.

This is not what Bentham intended for his afterlife. He wanted his body to be used for science and also brought to parties. He did partake in a college council meeting, but there is no record of his stuffed body attending any festivities at all until he was exhibited at the Met Breuer museum in New York City. He no doubt enjoyed the opening night gala, 186 years after his death.

Bentham's body, with waxen head, currently resides in the student center for all to see. The original head is shown separately, in a much more secure display case. I'm thinking it could be the inspiration for a new heist movie in the tradition of *Ocean's Eleven*—not the remake, but the original—and the reanimated bodies of Frank Sinatra and the Rat Pack would pull off the cranial caper.

Part of Jeremy Bentham's philosophy encompassed the concept of the carrot-and-the-stick approach to motivation. If you want a donkey to move, you can either offer her a carrot to lure her or whack her with a stick to get her moving. It's the same

---

* See the interlude "Things to Do When You're Dead."

with humans. You can be spurred on by punishment or motivated by a reward.

The carrot and the stick will both get the animal to move, but whipping will make it miserable, bruised, and untrusting. Donkeys motivated by carrots will be healthy and content and have good eyesight.

The donkey seems like a somewhat comical and ridiculous animal. In fact, the early Stoic philosopher Chrysippus fell into a fit of laughter when he spotted a donkey eating figs. He called out for his friends to give the beast some wine to wash down the fruit. Chrysippus laughed so hard at his own joke that he died. This doesn't seem especially amusing to me, but I guess in a time before memes you took your LOLz where you could.

There is a persistent image of the donkey as foolish. However, *equus asinus* is more than a braying, long-eared figure of fun. Humanity has a long and intimate association with donkeys, and they have insinuated themselves into our myths, culture, parables, and philosophy—sometimes as silly creatures, but often as heroes.

At the dawn of human history, donkeys enabled mobility. They carried pastoralists as they followed their herds, and traders as they brought distant goods and cultures and customs back home. The earliest Egyptian pharaohs were buried with donkeys. In Apuleius's *The Golden Ass*, the main character is changed for the better by his transformation into a humble *equus asinus*.

I think the other common name for them, ass, might have contributed to the image problem they now suffer. As for myself, I admire their qualities of strength and determination. How can you not love an animal that looks like a donkey?

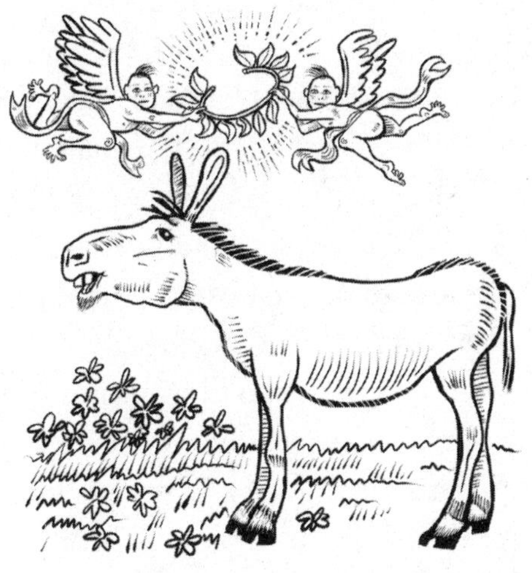

Proud to Be Called Jackass

A donkey, or ass, is a domesticated member of the equine family *equus africanus asinus*. A male donkey, or ass, is called a "jack," as in the generic name for a man, so a jackass is a male donkey. A female was once called a "she-ass," but the common term now is "jenny" or "jennet." When a jackass mates with a mare, or female horse, the offspring is a mule. A stallion that mates with a jenny will parent a hinny. If a male zebra should get amorous with a jenny, the result is called a zonkey, but if a jackass makes it with a lady zebra, you've got a zedonk. In the United States, east of the Mississippi River, *equus africanus asinus* is known as a donkey, but in the West, the name "burro" is more common, which is the Spanish word for donkey. Burrito, the food, literally means "little donkey," possibly because burritos have many ingredients, and donkeys can carry many different things on their backs.

A few years ago, your father asked what I wanted for my birthday and I told him I wanted a pair of donkeys. I mean, how can you resist the philosophical charm of a jackass? After some investigation, he informed me that "it's remarkably easy to find a used donkey." He located two fine fellows, full brothers, whose owner was an animal hoarder who could not afford to feed them.

Now we have a herd of used cows, a used dog, a few stray barn cats that wandered in, and two used donkeys. We don't call them rescues because we didn't have to rush into a burning fireworks factory and carry them out on our backs to save them. My friend Francis tells me that Los Angeles is infested with cars bearing a paw print sticker that asks, "Who Rescued Who?" I don't know, but I do know who's bragging about it.

I wanted to name the donkey brothers after my two favorite philosophers, Epictetus and Jeremy Bentham, but you and your father insisted it was bad luck to rename a donkey. Jake and Mason, as they remain named, are equine charisma on the hoof. Our donkey brothers offer us charming companionship and an opportunity to employ the nicer half of Bentham's theory of the carrot and the stick. When we move these stubborn siblings from the pasture to the stable, carrots are the carrots, and we forgo the sticks.

Small rewards keep us focused, keep our eye on the ball, and keep us moving, step by step, toward our goals. I think regular rewards are a better motivator than small smacks. Once when we were on vacation in Vermont, a stranger approached me and complimented you: "Your son is so cool and mature for a four-year-old." I explained that we rewarded your good behavior, rather than punishing you when you acted out. I think this approach has worked spectacularly. Another advantage of motivation through small rewards is that you can give them to yourself. I don't think it's nearly as effective to give yourself a punch when you need to get off your keister and take the recycling to the barn.

Small-carrot goals help us create the momentum we need to chase bigger goals as we go on. Small carrots are easier to achieve, and then we build on them. With every small carrot, we can see ourselves getting smarter, getting better, getting stronger. This offers a sense of accomplishment, which increases our confidence and inspires us to scale up. One foot in front of the other. Small goals add up. They are achievable and flexible. Your goals will change over time, but the experience you gain from achieving small carrots will give the confidence to change direction, as all skills are transferable.

Some goals are enormous, like writing an epistolary book about classical wisdom. The majority of our goals are smaller objectives through which we aspire to slay the demons of mediocrity. My old buddy and armchair philosopher Kevin Ward and I shared a scrappy beach shack on Shelter Island for years. On weekends, we'd imbibe a "psychological cocktail" together, the drink you have with your bros before you go to a party. Then we got dressed while listening to music, hopped on the boat, and water-skied naked in a phosphorescent tide. Before making landfall, we put our party rags back on and walked up the dock to the party in seawater-scented clothes. Kevin insisted that all the experiences we had on the way to a party were inevitably more fun than the actual party. He called this his "Theory of the Ostensible Destination."

The "ostensible destination" awakens you to live in the moment, yet offers a driving force to move you forward. It is a decoy. When we set goals and move toward them, we gain the most from the process, not crossing the finish line. We spend most of our lives in between states of aspiration, between the you of today and the future you. What happens in the meantime is your life. Like the orange edible root that is dangled in front of a donkey, we all need our small-carrot goals to keep us inspired and in motion. The carrot is the ostensible destination.

Small carrots awaken us to live in the present, print memories from our past, and fuel our drive to future success. They are bite-size goals that allow us to see tangible results and attain the satisfaction and accomplishment of a hard-won victory. Progress is evident, and that reinforces the goal. The road to success is paved by a series of small carrots strung together. The alchemy of small carrots is that they convert pessimism into optimism into vitamin K.

In Their Hooves

The Greek island of Santorini was formed from the eruptions of an ancient, powerful volcano. The massive explosion in 1600 BC was one of the largest in history and may have led to the legend of Atlantis, a powerful island civilization that disappeared beneath the waves. The island today is craggy with steep cliffs, and visitors who wish to ascend from the port to the main town of Fira face a climb of 586 steps. Local entrepreneurs have provided an alternative to footsore tourists in the form of donkeys who carry the lazy lookie-loos up and down. These poor asses are often beaten by their owners and suffer from being made to carry corpulent foreigners in the hot sun. The organization In Their Hooves advocates for donkeys and urges tourists to take note of whether these noble animals are being well treated. The Greek government has banned riders over 220 pounds, and TripAdvisor is filled with questions from creative travelers who want to know whether they can weigh in naked to limbo under the limit. These folks really want to eat their baklava and have their donkey ride, too. I think next time we ascend to Fira, I will keep the welfare of the donkeys in mind and travel by "shank's mare"—on foot.

* * *

You have lofty goals for yourself. One of them is to play college hockey. It will be challenging to get there, if you do get there. Reaching your big goal requires a lot of smaller steps on the way. You need to study well, practice hard, work out, and hone your skills. You sacrifice time with your friends and spend weeks every summer attending goalie camp while they are hanging out with girls at the beach. Reward yourself for these steps with a small carrot. After a long skate, give yourself a break and play EA Sports NHL or check in with the knuckleheads on Spittin' Chiclets.

Some mad geniuses work by setting lofty goals and maniacally working toward them with no intermediate steps. These visionaries see beyond the mortal limits of our 20/20 vision. Elon Musk is determined to get to Mars, whatever it takes. Most of us don't work like this. My small-carrot goal is to invent chocolate dentures, so even when you're eating root vegetables it tastes like a Mars Bar. I'll get rich, and only then turn my sights toward the Red Planet.

The most important thing you can do is act. Newton's Law of Inertia says that it takes energy to get you in motion, but once you get started, you'll keep going. You may go slowly, but you'll be on your way. The only failure is when you don't try. "The beginning of the work is the most important part of the work," as Plato said.

I have a friend who's redoing a room in her house into a meditation and yoga room. "Do you even do yoga?" I asked. "No, but I will when I get the room," she said. She's never going to do yoga. The room is an excuse. Epictetus said, "If you are careless and lazy now and keep putting things off and always deferring the day after which you will attend to yourself, you will not notice that you are making no progress, but you will live and die as someone quite ordinary."

Decide on your goal and select a small-carrot step to take. The baby carrots will keep you moving, and on the way, you embrace the beauty and chaos of the journey. I love writing, but it's very easy to put it off, delay, procrastinate, jump in the lake, or go out for a coffee with a pal. To motivate myself, I find a small carrot. If I sit down to write, I get to listen to old-school love songs. If I get stuck, I make myself a cup of tea as a reward for what I did do. Once I have scribbled a few pages, I get to take a walk. One of my carrots is the reward of strolling down to the barnyard to give real carrots to Jake and Mason. When I despair about getting a book written, I think of the stubborn nature I see in our donkeys.

Marshmallows can be a carrot, too. The only exercise I enjoy is walking, but when it's too cold or rainy, I stay inside. I hired you to be my personal trainer, and to motivate me, you tied a string to your drone and a marshmallow to the string. You would fly the drone around the house so I would chase it to get in some of my daily goal of ten thousand steps. It was working great until I got to the pantry and sat down with the open bag of marshmallows.

Small carrots can be something you give yourself or something offered by others, like gratitude and respect—a pat on the back, an "'atta boy," a reward. Hand out small carrots to others when you can. In the words of Reverend John Watson, "Be pitiful [that is, compassionate], for every man is fighting a hard battle." And of course, for those who like them, actual mini-carrots can be a fine motivator.

Your goal is to discover a few things that you excel in, and then jump in and make it your business to do your best, one small carrot at a time. To not utilize your talents is to disregard the gifts that you have in your power. This is how you waste an opportunity; this is how you throw away your shot. This is the easiest way to fail. As the writer Russell Green said, "Heaven is the place where the donkey finally catches up with his carrot; hell is the eternity while he waits for it."

You are my twenty-four-carrot lad,

Mum

10

HOMO STUPIDUS TO HOMO SAPIENS

Dear Slim,

You're an athlete, and you work hard to gain muscle and keep fit. You see old geezers sweating their cojones off in our local gym, bench pressing to get rid of their man-boobs. Brian Zembic is a feral wild man who went the opposite direction. He is a high-stakes gambler who once, on a bet, lived in his buddy's bathroom for a week. He slept on a bench in Central Park with twenty thousand dollars in his pocket to get a payout. A friend offered him a cool hundred grand if he got breast implants and kept them for a year. Zembic won the cost of the surgically implanted sweater kittens by betting on a backgammon game with his doctor. He made it through the year, collected on the bet, and decided to keep the new funbags. "They grew on me," he said, and he treasured his jugs for sixteen more years.*

* Zembic's teenage daughter eventually made him remove his double-D double lattes.

Larry Walters had always dreamed of being a pilot. He was rejected by the Air Force because of poor eyesight, but the desire for flight still soared in his heart. On a sunny summer day, he attached forty-five helium-filled weather balloons to a cheap aluminum lawn chair. He packed beer, sandwiches, a CB radio, a camera, and a pellet gun. His friends cut the tether on his chair, which he had dubbed the Inspiration I, and he slipped the surly bonds of Earth. Walters soared to sixteen thousand feet and was spotted by the startled crews of passing jets before he was coaxed into heading back to Earth by air traffic control. He shot the balloons out one by one and touched down safely.

Annie Edson Taylor was a retired schoolteacher without a pension. She needed money to live on in her golden years, so she conceived a spectacular scheme to feather her nest. On October 24, 1901, she climbed into a barrel floating in the Niagara River. Her friends cast it adrift, and Annie became the first person to go over Niagara Falls in a barrel and live. It was her sixty-third birthday. Sadly, her amazing feat didn't bring her the financial windfall she'd hoped for. But resourceful Annie never stopped trying to hustle up a nest egg.

These weren't the pranks of wayward, hormonal, risk-taking youth. Big-Breasted Brian; Lawnchair Larry; and Annie, Queen of the Mist, were all fully grown adults. They provide an invaluable reminder that age is no guarantee of maturity. We can celebrate these bon vivants for their daring and their entertainment value, while at the same time recognizing that they are absolutely barking mad. I imagine that these folks have not just an inner child but also an inner teenager who sometimes steers the ship.

The scientific name for the human species is Homo sapiens, bestowed on us by Swedish botanist Carolus Linnaeus in 1753. The phrase is Latin for "wise man." I think it is a pretty cocky moniker for all of humanity, especially the goons you watch on Barstool Sports. When the first skeleton of Neanderthal man was unearthed, German biologist Ernst Haeckel proposed calling the newly identified species "Homo stupidus." The title didn't stick, but it seems like an equally apt name for our own species.

For many, immaturity is a choice, a way of living, and not necessarily a defect. Growing up is no guarantee that your childish spirit will be extinguished. This is why you need a framework, a sense of morals, a personal code, and a philosophy that will help pilot you to become the person you aspire to be, at any age.

We recently celebrated your sixteenth birthday. On Uranus, which takes eighty-four of our years to orbit the sun, you're a nineteen-day-old infant. In dog years, you're eighty and in frisky and playful shape for your age. It takes a lobster seven years to gain one pound, and then it gains a pound a year for the rest of its arthropod life. Based on your poundage, in lobster years, you're a tasty 174. In Greece, you're age one at birth. So, after your first twelve months of life, you'd celebrate your second birthday. Congratulations, Jack, you're actually seventeen and eligible for an unrestricted New York driver's license!

Our civilization has been celebrating the birthdays of young people after age twelve for millennia, yet it is a modern convention to anoint the time between childhood and adulthood with a specific title. The word "teenager" is a relatively new term. It was coined in the early 1900s, but it didn't spread in popular culture until the early 1940s.

We now know that adolescence extends far beyond your nineteenth birthday. Brain development continues into the mid-twenties. But for simplicity, I'll call the span between thirteen and twenty-four the "teenage years."

When the US economy shifted from farming to industrialization, families moved closer to cities. There were no child labor laws and young kids were exploited as weavers, cobblers, sandhogs, and oyster shuckers. The view was that once you went down to the salt mine, you were no longer a child.

When Are You an Adult?

Youngest age to be tried as an adult, in the Middle Ages: seven
For a bar mitzvah: thirteen
Amish children can work in sawmills: after eighth grade
Can get a part-time job in the United States: fourteen
Youngest age of consent in the United States: sixteen
Can go to an R-rated movie by yourself: seventeen

Voting age and military draft age: eighteen
Age of majority in South Korea and Canada: nineteen
Legal drinking age in the United States: twenty-one
Can rent a car: twenty-five. Car companies side with neuroscience and have determined that age twenty-five is when the prefrontal cortex is fully developed, meaning you're less likely to get into a wreck while driving like a crazy person.

* * *

The Great Depression and then the Fair Labor Laws of 1938 emancipated children from the workforce. At the same time, compulsory public education doubled the number of high-school students. Teenagers spent more time in school, more time with their peers, and they created their own style and slang away from the prying eyes of their parents. With kids in school longer, marriage was delayed. The spread of cars gave this new social group a way to meet each other and have sex. We have Henry Ford to thank for back-seat romance.

There is a limiting belief that the teen years are a period that parents and children must endure, like a dozen-year dental visit. In the words of William Galvin, "Mother Nature is providential. She gives us twelve years to develop a love for our kids before turning them into teenagers." The teenage years can feel like a purgatory, like you are restless souls waiting for your lives to begin. Students can't wait to graduate. Adolescents can't wait to gain independence. Parents can't wait to get that bedroom for a home office.

The period of adolescence is a time of spectacular change. Between ages thirteen and twenty-four, humans are young, strong, bendy, and healthy, and yet this demographic has the highest rate of accidental death. Teens are in their physical prime, but the brain's prefrontal cortex, which helps regulate impulsive behavior, hasn't fully developed. Which is why the words "Hold my beer and watch this" are often followed by the scream, "Call 911!"*

Adolescence is not just a circus of misadventure, acne vulgaris, and untimely boners. It is an intense period of growth. This is an amazing, challenging, and thrilling dozen years.

Your teenage brain is not a smaller and less wrinkly adult brain; it's a distinctly different operating system. Between ages thirteen and twenty-four, your brain develops and changes in spectacularly important ways. In these dozen years, you'll acquire vital skills such as learning to connect and create friendships and romantic relationships, how to navigate taking risks, and how to leave home and become a citizen of the world.

Discard the idea that the teenage years are a transitional period, the waiting room before your journey begins. The starter pistol has been fired and the race of your life has begun. Take off running and enjoy it with all its hurdles.

We often blame teenage behavior on "raging hormones." It is true that there are gallons of hormones coursing through you, but it's not just these chemicals that shape the teen years. Your brain has reached its largest size, and it has many more neurons than an adult's. You're exploding with brainpower. The squishy blob between your ears with the weight of a bag of potatoes, this guinea pig–sized orb, this is what makes you human.

---

* "Rantipole" means a rude, unruly young person. The word comes from "rant," meaning wild, and "pole," meaning head.

The prefrontal cortex is the CEO of your brain, responsible for planning, prioritizing, modulating mood, and controlling impulses. It helps you engage in "sober second thoughts" before you act. Because it's still under construction, young people are more likely to take risks without considering the consequences. It's the last part of your brain to mature, yet it's the most important. The immature prefrontal cortex is what makes young people act like a pack of wolverines. I wonder why nature did that.

Adult and teen brains work differently. When I am nagging you to death, I need to remind myself, and you, that we are functioning on two different operating systems. Adults think with the wisdom of a matured prefrontal cortex, the brain's rational decision center. Teens process information with the amygdala, the emotional part of the brain. Your nucleus accumbens, which rewards and reinforces pleasurable things like sex, BASE jumping, and bocce, is enlarged during adolescence. This is why you feel things so passionately.

Your young brain has many more cells than an adult's, and it's constantly rewiring itself. The connections you're making now, your friends, and your tastes in fine art (ha!) will stay with you throughout your life. This is why we never stop loving the music we listened to as teens. I formed a barnacle-like attachment to Johnny Cash, Al Green, and Herb Alpert (who were not actually popular during my youth, but I liked them anyway). For you, your future holds an endless series of car rides during which you try to convince your own kid that Flo Rida is really the bee's knees.

Your intensely firing neurons can be tough to deal with, but they're also a superpower. You are passionate, driven, fiercely curious. These are things adults must work toward, but to you they come naturally. As Seneca wrote, "Hang on to your youthful enthusiasms—you'll be able to use them better when you're older."

To adults, teenagers can seem like they have their own *omertà*—moody, introspective, sullen. It is normal for humans to look inward as they grow. Teenagers are taking what they have learned from their parents, mentors, teachers, and coaches and building on it to form their own philosophy and refine their morals. They are awakening to the complexity and disappointments of the world and are taking the time they need to grapple with adult reality. We grown-ups have already gone through this process, and it seems we forgot entirely what it was like. The job of teens is to push boundaries, develop interests, and create a framework of core traits and the backbone of independence.

Parents may think teens are shunning them, but it's only because they like to hang out with one another. Teenagers are one another's emotional support mammals. The friends they're making in school will likely be friends for life. Goofing off and joking around with friends prepares them for adulthood more than the SATs.

In the media, adolescent males are portrayed as trained chimps without the training. Mothers are portrayed as the wet blankets, always the enemies of fun. It is true that the dirty clothes in your "bachelor chambers" look as though a body is hiding under your bed. Without me chewing a hole in your shorts to get the pile in the wash, you'd adopt it as a brother. When I remind you to do the laundry, you call me "Saggy Naggy" and do your funny sing-song voice: "Eat your vegetables, wear a sweater." I laugh. We know how to push each other's buttons because we installed them, but we don't have to be antagonistic. Humor is a good lubricant when we are grinding each other's gears. Parents have to evolve and grow along with their kids as we blaze through the stages of life together.

Adolescence is a steeplechase of physical, intellectual, emotional, and hormonal development. I understand that the chemicals in your body are metamorphosing you into a man in front of my eyes. Testosterone is making you grow up and grow away. Understanding what is going on in one another's brains and bodies will create a more peaceful and productive progression.

That said, I know that while you are under my menstrual cramp dictatorship, the sound of my voice asking whether you'd like a smoothie goes through you like a dental drill hitting a nerve. It's not a personality flaw in you or me. It's evolution's way of using testosterone as the rocket fuel to power you on your own wild, independent flight. Mothers are righteous and awesome, but you need to become your own man. Understanding that nature created this powerful secretion to loosen the bond can take the sting out of those potentially hurtful moments.

I know parents who don't eat breakfast with their children. They prefer exercising to eating, and they want to avoid scrapping with their offspring first thing in the morning. In our family, breakfast is the meal we always share together. You've come up with some of your best jokes over toast and OJ.

When we are not cracking wise, we read. We always have the sports section of the *New York Times* on the table, as well as works of classical philosophy by Marcus Aurelius, Aristotle, and of course, the Sharon Lebell translation of Epictetus. You've always been encouraged to read as much as you like while masticating your Eggs James Bond.*

We wanted you to have a grounding in these philosophers, but we knew that you weren't going to pick it up if we TED talked your ears off. You can't explain Stoicism when you're yelling. It is imparted by training, taking action, learning from example, and reading in the breakfast nook. Stoicism is the antidote to naggy parenting and to teenage tantrums. Stoic philosophy has created a shorthand for us to discuss topics that are hard to talk about, like anxiety and worry about getting into college, about life goals and finding your purpose. I recall a conversation where you reminded me that Epictetus said, "Cease worrying about things that are beyond our power or our will." Greek fire ignited in my heart when you said that.

Your teenage years are the time when you begin to set your goals and decide who you want to be. You're charting out how you want to live like a cartographer. You can't get where you want to go without a map. As an emerging adult, society seems to feel that it has a hand-delivered invitation to tell you what to do. We urge young people to grow up, but we are really telling them to stop growing. Just reach a reasonable plateau and settle there—a predictable, unthreatening, and unchanging plateau. Don't do that. Here is the dynamite to blow that up: read philosophy. It will be your atlas.

Epictetus is my number one Stoic sage, and I have downloaded his words into my brain. I read his work every day like

* This was the first recipe I taught you. The debonair secret agent ate lots of eggs, and in the short story "The Plaza Hotel," he gives his personal recipe: scramble eggs in butter, serve over buttered toast, pour melted butter over the whole mess. A group of doctors once calculated that if Bond were a real person, he would have died of cirrhosis (from the martinis) and high cholesterol by age fifty-nine.

a devotional. He was born a slave, and his teenage years were spent in bondage. His core Stoic principle is that we can't control what happens; we can only control how we respond. His message is especially relevant for the over-the-top, emotional responses that come with the territory at your age.

Epictetus focuses on the responsibility of each individual to live the best life possible by following his principles. He teaches us to keep an active, radiant mind no matter what life throws at us. I think you've benefited from keeping this wisdom in your thoughts. A Stoic is someone who turns ideas into action, pain into transformation, and mistakes into education. The simplicity and clarity of Stoic philosophy will bring you peace and tranquility in tough times and good. It's a way of life, not only an academic discipline.

You assemble your own life, action by action. But you can't do it all by yourself. You couldn't find a better wingman than Epictetus.

Studying philosophy is a lifelong pursuit, and I still have a long way to go. I have a prankish, middle-aged tomboy nature. When I get together with my friends, you see us turning on a cheap champagne fountain and filling it with boozy eggnog. When digging through our couch cushions, you're likely to find long-lost fart machines. I recall the time my friends Lori and Lynn and I went to the Bargain Barn, bought vintage ski suits, and wore them all weekend while we played drinking games and pretended we were at a Swiss ski lodge. I think you disapproved. You are more like your dad: responsible, driven, and introspective.

I don't know whether Greta Thunberg is a reader of Epictetus. I do know that her leadership in the movement to address climate change is proof that just as adults like Big-Breasted

Brian can be immature, teenagers can act with great wisdom. Freddie and Truus Oversteegen, Dutch sisters who hunted Nazis in World War II, show us that teenagers can act with great courage. John Lewis, the civil rights leader, preached his first sermon at age fifteen and met with Dr. Martin Luther King Jr. at eighteen. Teenagers can act for justice, too.

I don't demand that you do any of these things, but I won't be surprised if you do something great. The pride I radiate from being your mum must be the way Clark Kent felt when he was eavesdropping in the newsroom and heard his coworkers marveling at the latest feat of Superman. My goal for you is to continue being a spectacular credit to humanity. In your short life, you've proven that Carolus Linnaeus was right to name us Homo sapiens, as opposed to Ernst Haeckl's Homo stupidus.

Every day is the prime of your life,

Mum

—INTERLUDE—

The Four Cardinal Virtues

"Arete" is a Greek word meaning, roughly, "moral excellence." A person who has *arete* is living life to the fullest and using all her capacities to fulfill her purpose.

Marcus Aurelius urged us, "Waste no more time arguing about what a good man should be—be one." Good men (and women) embody the four cardinal virtues that Stoic philosophy esteems most highly: wisdom, courage, moderation, and justice. These virtues are your moral guidelines as you soar through life.

Wisdom. Philosophy means love of wisdom. Wisdom is knowledge that guides and inspires our actions. Live according to the standards you set for yourself. If you compare yourself to others and find yourself better, that is vanity. If you compare yourself to others and feel you don't measure up, that's depressing. As Marcus Aurelius said, "It never ceases to amaze me: we love ourselves more than other people but care more about their opinion than our own." Wisdom is comparing yourself only to yourself and to the standards you aspire to.

Courage. It takes guts to commit to your purpose. Courage is the moxie to grab the day by the neck and kiss it. Courage is not restricted to conquering the emotion of fear; it's the strength of character to rise above things that may drag us down. It's approaching life with confidence and following through with difficult and demanding tasks. It is the virtue that gets you off Instagram and out into the world. Character is choosing courage over complacency.

Moderation. My father always said that life was like the three interlocking rings on the can of Ballantine beer. One represented family and friends, one your work, and the third your spiritual life. The rings are all equally positioned, and if you allow one to dominate, you will be out of whack. Aristotle called this virtue of moderation the "golden mean." Moderation is found between excess and deficiency: for example, too much courage leads to recklessness, but too little, to cowardice.

Justice. For the Stoics, this idea goes far beyond courts of law. The wise philosopher Donald Robertson, whom I am lucky to count as a friend, wrote that in Stoicism, justice "is a less formal concept than the English word implies and really refers to social virtue in quite a broad sense." Justice "entails the exercise of wisdom, kindness, and fairness in our relationships with others both individually and collectively." Justice is doing good in the world.

~

11

READ YOURSELF A NEW BRAIN

Dear Jack,

Your body consists of the scaffolding of your skeleton, the sinewy fretwork of your muscles, gallons of water, plasma, and hormones, and the gases oxygen, nitrogen, and methane. The interlocking puzzle of internal organs is upholstered in yards of flexible material that is your skin. This glorious edifice is crowned by a hard, resilient bucket that protects the three-pound orb of gelatinous slop that makes up the control center, which compiles information through the seven holes in your skull. This is a wonder.

The most amazing creation in the universe is your body and the most astonishing part is inside your skull. Your brain is 80 percent water and the rest is a 50/50 split between fat and protein. These ingredients that make you think and make you *you* can be found in the cold-cut drawer of our refrigerator, yet they create the most complex masterwork in the universe.

These are your raw materials. We are composed of components as simple as a baloney sandwich. The true miracle of life is that we are made of this humble stuff, yet our thoughts are divinely transcendent. These are wondrous gifts. What you do with these powers will be your gift to the world.

You are the apex of creation. Even when you are sleeping or have parked your brain in front of the Xbox, you are the pinnacle of a long chain of evolution. You are a universe of connected networks. You are a constellation of unexceptional molecules, yet the human brain is the brightest instrument in existence.

My body and brain are vastly different from your corpus and operating system.

Jack, you live with a mom who's been living with complex medical issues and a degenerative neurological disease for your whole life. You never knew the sporty, active, healthy version of me. My neuropathy impacts fine motor skills. It feels like I'm wearing a catcher's mitt on each hand. I can't open jars or tie shoes. Belts, buttons, locks, and keys are exercises in frustration. I've had to figure out a way to live in acceptance of these deficits, but I understand it is only natural for everyone else to feel impatient. I've become a master at the magician's trick of misdirection, diverting attention with a wisecrack while I fumble with a zipper. I don't even realize I've left every drawer in the house open until your father comes home and closes them all. He says it's like living with a poltergeist.

When you were about four, I started a conversation with you about why small things that are easy for the other moms take a frustratingly long time for me. I gently asked you whether you noticed that I'm not like the other moms. You replied, "Because you're pretty?" I think you were polishing my apple, because we walked to preschool most days with the stunning Brooke Shields and her two gorgeous daughters.

After I informed you about my disabilities, such as having no feeling in my hands and feet, you began to look out for me.

We were at your aunt Kate's house, and I was leaning on the kitchen island. She has an electric range, and my hand was inches from a hot element. You were not even in kindergarten, but you had the presence of mind to walk over and silently and gently move my hand away from the heat source.

I worry that my deficits and illness will affect you, but you are always patient with me. The other day we were driving to Arethusa Farms to get the eggnog you and your father like so much. While at the wheel, I had my down jacket on and wanted to get it off. I started thrashing around like a gaffed whale, shouting, "I'm heating up!" You calmly helped me out of my jacket, probably saving both our lives in the process.

I believe I best convey my thoughts and wisdom through my numb left hand. You don't have a sibling, and if a clown swings me around by the ankles and my head rams into a circus tentpole, these letters are my backup in the event you don't get me as a mom as you grow into manhood. I want to share my love, my spiritual faith, and my admiration for Stoic philosophy. I want to impart this wisdom as you cultivate your inner man.

You gather knowledge through all of your senses, and they are all important. Yet most people downplay the sense of smell. It is the one most people would give up if they had to play sensory roulette and lose one. A stunning 53 percent of people under age thirty would sacrifice their sense of smell rather than give up their smartphone.*

Smell is much more important to us than we appreciate; it's the underdog of senses. When we take in an odor through our blowholes, the information goes directly to the olfactory cortex. This piece of equipment is located next to the hippocampus, the seahorse-shaped part of our brain where our memories are shaped. Neurologists believe this is why particular aromas create powerful memories in us.

The medical term for someone with an impaired nose is "anosmatic." Anosmia is the total loss of the sense of smell and hyposmia is partial loss. Between 2 and 5 percent of the people in the world suffer from some degree of smelling loss, but total anosmia is quite rare.

Our buddy George lost his sense of smell when he was a teenager. He was walking with his hands stuck in the back pockets of his pants and tripped and hit his head on a manhole cover. His tight jeans clenched his hands like Chinese finger traps, and he couldn't pull them out to break the fall. His sense of smell came back, decades later, just in time to change his twins' nappies.

The short straw in the nasal disability category is cacosmia. This is a condition where everything smells feculent.

---

* One in ten would even sacrifice a finger rather than their phone.

A brain lesion and years of chemotherapy left me with total anosmia. Because I can't smell a thing, I am extra-vigilant about cleaning your hockey equipment: skates, pads, gloves, blockers, helmets, and, of course, nut cups. Nobody wants to parent the smelly kid. My sister Kate remarked, "I don't think the Yankee Candle Company is going to come out with a fragrance called 'Goalie Glove' or 'Winter Seasonal Hockey Sock.'"

The deodorizing sprays you can buy in the laundry aisle don't cut it. You didn't want to smell like flowers or a spring meadow. I needed the hard stuff. I went online and found something called Monkey Cage Cleaner, which is what zookeepers use to hose down their primate enclosures. I sprayed down your gear generously. I guess I should have read the instructions first, which urged me to "Dilute before using." I couldn't smell it, but I could see the stink lines emanating off your jersey, the way Charles Schultz drew the character Pig-Pen. The Monkey Cage Cleaner, I was informed, smelled even worse than the inside of your skates. I'll stick to soaps and deodorizers meant for humans from now on, although I am sorry I don't get to tell my sisters that I wash my son's gear with zoological products.

As a child, you took on a protective, watchful role but also a "smellful" role. I can't sense certain dangers like gas, or smoke, or stinky cheese. Perhaps your senses are heightened because we spend so much time together. You're like my support animal . . . except a biped.

Dr. Gary Beauchamp, the president emeritus of the Monell Chemical Senses Center in Philadelphia, noted that "people who lose their sense of smell are usually astounded at how much pleasure it takes out of their lives. We depend on smell for interpreting the world but also, no less crucially, for getting pleasure from it." I am okay with where I am at; I've made peace with it.

In fact, I forget that my nose doesn't work (except when a friend casually remarks that something "doesn't pass the smell test"). I'm grateful to my brain for being so resilient. As Epictetus said, "He is a wise man who does not grieve for the things which he has not, but rejoices for those which he has."

Though I have accepted that my blowholes are out of business, I miss certain smells. I didn't know what the top of your head smelled like when you were a baby. I missed it. I miss the intoxicating vapors of Gus's French toast at the Bonbonniere. I even miss disgusting smells like the plume of subway steam billowing from bright orange construction vents. I miss the smell of the Subway sandwich shop on 8th Street. My pal Jon Stewart said, "Subway smells like a loaf of bread farted."*

Disgust is an evolutionary reaction that protects us from harm. We feel disgust at things that may be dangerous. Females experience disgust more easily than males because they are protecting their bodies and the offspring they may carry inside them. Disgust is a behavioral immune system that keeps pathogens out.

Both male and female teenagers are more sensitive to disgust than adults, but as a rule of thumb, it's boys who are disgusting and girls who are disgusted. Our sense of revulsion at foul smells declines as we age because our fertility declines. Geezers are harder to gross out—their behavioral immune system weakens past reproductive age. I'm glad to have you around because your heightened sense of disgust helps me avoid the sinister fumes of salmonella-riddled chicken.

The feeling of disgust is a learning experience. It's a warning, and if you follow the Stoics, you can examine that feeling

* Why did a huge food conglomerate name a smelly sandwich shop after a smelly underground train?

and decide how it serves you. If you are grossed out by the smell of cow pats and donkey doo in our pasture, you can accept it and walk on. If you are repelled by the clams casino I'm cooking up, you can use that feeling to rocket yourself away from the *fruits de mer* and leave more for me. Thank you!

Just as there would be no scent of roses without the funk of fertilizer and no beauty without the carbuncles and warts of ugliness, there would be no intelligence without stupidity. Humanity's secret weapons are disgust and stupidity, the stepbrothers of evolution. We should all be grateful to nature for giving us the involuntary reaction of disgust that protects our body and brain. We should be thankful for human stupidity, which inoculates us against future missteps.

We are at our pinnacle as a species. Don't we owe it to our ancestors who lived through disgustingly stupid times like the Middle Ages to maximize our existence? These poor peasants washed their faces with urine, drank puppy blood as an attempt to cure acne, and ate raw cat meat in a futile effort to relieve asthma. If we don't optimize our brainpower now, we would be ingrates to our ancestors, all those disgusting, smelly, rancid, stupid, imbecilic, domestic-pet-nibbling relatives, who are the deep roots of humanity's family tree.

Manuscript Curses

In the Middle Ages, nobody read books because there were so few to read. Before the invention of the printing press, producing a new book was an intensive and time-consuming affair. Teams of scribes would painstakingly copy a volume word by word. This was also before central heating and electricity, so the scribes suffered eye strain and chilblains. These men labored hard to spread the knowledge contained in books and were not happy to think that their work might have ale spilled on it or come to misadventure. So, their copies included something extra: curses on anyone who harmed the tome. "Whoever steals this book, let him die the death: Let him be frizzled with pain, may the falling sickness rage within him. May he be broken on the wheel or hanged," reads one such curse. I can only imagine what these scribes would have said about the dog-eared, marked-up volumes in my library.

* * *

Stupidity spurs us to take action. It is a resource—we can reflect on our own (and others') past stupid acts, to become less so. Writer Nicolas Chamfort put it this way: "A man should swallow a toad every morning so that he might meet with nothing more disgusting during the rest of the day." Get the stupid out of the way early.

According to Cunningham's Law, the best way to get the right answer to a question is to post the wrong answer online. Stupidity can lead us to knowledge. The Information Age offers a great opportunity to be intelligent, but it's also an opportunity to be stupid. We live in the golden age of stupidity. We are the highest, most intelligent beings, yet our stupidity is incredibly resilient in the face of valuable lessons of life. We are profoundly brilliant yet remarkably dumb. We want new knowledge, information we didn't know, brilliant facts, and ephemera to dazzle and amaze. We are so excited by shiny new things that we overlook the wisdom of the past.

I am not immune to the charms of quirky and unusual information. How else would I know that the average person farts fourteen times a day and laughs seventeen times a day? How could I have learned about US Government Standard Bathroom Malodor? This horrible stench that mimics the smell of an uncleaned latrine was brewed up for use in weapons-grade stink bombs. Or that Christianity made the continent of Europe fetid? When Christians exiled the Greek and Roman gods, they tossed the Greco-Roman tradition of bathing out with the bathwater. Early Christians believed that cleansing the body was a pagan rite and ungodly. It wasn't until the Renaissance that water-based rituals reappeared.

Our dinner conversations would be less lively if I didn't read all day. In ancient Rome, funeral clowns called "archimimes" were hired to follow the coffin and mimic the dead person. The belief was that the archimimes would placate the spirits and mug a laugh from the grieving relatives.

I've always been fascinated by unusual words and phrases and their etymology. What about whipping boys, you might ask? I can answer that. In the fifteenth and sixteenth centuries, the job of educating royalty was tricky. Tutors enforced princely study habits with corporal punishment, yet the belief in the Divine Right of Kings stated that kings were appointed by God. Disciplining a son of a king was problematic because tutors were not worthy of punishing God-given royalty. The solution was to nominate whipping boys. An innocent kid sat next to the prince, and when the future king put a tack on the tutor's chair or claimed that the royal dog ate his homework, the prince's human punching bag got walloped.

The whipping boy was appointed from a noble family and educated with the future king. The hope was that the prince and the whipping boy would become pals and this tight bond would instill compassion. It was an inspiration for the prince to model good behavior and study diligently for the whipping boy's sake. When they graduated, the bruised and beaten lad would often be granted a title and a royal estate. I'm not sure this information will be of much practical use to you, but it will make you a good raconteur at a party.

I enjoy my excursions into unusual history and offbeat science, but I make my home with Stoic philosophy. I become less stupid by mixing current information with classical wisdom. Epictetus wrote that "books are the training weights of the mind"; I consider my mental physique to be extremely well sculpted, while I have the muscle tone of a raw clam. Jack, you are in peak physical condition, and you are developing your mind as well.

Your school is academically rigorous, but education goes beyond homework and standardized tests. It is an openness to learning from the world. Thomas More remarked that "one of the greatest problems of our time is that many are schooled but few are educated." Books are a potent dietary source of brain sustenance and can make up for the nutritional deficits in your formal education. I grew up in a house full of sports balls rather than books, but I lived in the local library. I read myself a new brain.

As Woodrow Wilson said, "I not only use all the brain I have, but all that I can borrow." At the library, I borrow brains. When I look at our bookcases filled with volumes, I think of the words of Gilbert Highet, "These are not books, lumps of lifeless paper, but minds alive on the shelves."

The astronomer, scientist, and pope-botherer Galileo Galilei wrote that reading is almost like a superpower in its ability to connect us with distant people and places we may not see in our lifetime. Galileo wrote this in the late 1500s, four hundred years before the Marvel Cinematic Universe.

The Genius of Galileo

Galileo dedicated his whole being to research and discovery. He was a polymath and philosopher who remarked that wine is "sunlight, held together by water." Despite his many accomplishments, he fell out with the pope of Rome and was accused of heresy because of his scientific belief that the Earth revolves around the sun. He was put under house arrest, but while locked down, he didn't nurse a pope-hat-sized grudge. Instead, he devoted his time to writing two more masterworks. He went blind and lived in chronic pain, yet he composed a work that earned him the nickname "the father of modern physics." When Galileo died in 1642 at age seventy-seven, Pope Urban VII put a stop to his burial in a mausoleum next to the tombs of his father and ancestors in the Basilica of Santa Croce. Instead, he was planted in a small chapel off the main church. Nearly 100 years later, he was reburied in the Basilica. During his disinterment, three fingers and a tooth were taken from his remains. The fingers are presently on exhibition at the Museo Galileo in Florence, where we visited them. His middle finger is the one on display. Let's think about that.

* * *

Make a plan for your reading. You have a plan for your workouts and a schedule for school. When you have a plan and intention, you make the most out of your resources, out of your time, out of your life.

A polymath isn't a parrot with a calculator. It is a person who takes an interest in many and varied subjects and educates themself widely. The way to be a polymath is to be a lifelong learner, and this is the plan I have made for myself. It is what I hope for you.

I create a reading list from friends' recommendations, book reviews, and references in other books. The paradox of choice tells us that too much of anything leaves us paralyzed and unable to make a decision. A pile of books on the nightstand is a graveyard of good intentions.* I keep a handwritten list of what books I want to read next. Books can jump the line, but it's important to keep some kind of order.

Reading books, unlike social media posts, inspires your brain to engage in critical thinking and make connections. These connections create new neural pathways, making you smarter and more quick-thinking. Connecting to new ideas, words, facts, and philosophies increases your cognitive reserve and makes your mind resilient.

It's never too late to become less stupid. I am proof of that. As Socrates noted, "Employ your time in improving yourself by other men's writings, so that you shall gain easily what others have labored hard for."

Ben Franklin said that "an investment in knowledge pays the best interest"; your intellectual capital will be the best reward for the investment of your time. What you read today will be useful to you for seventy more years. Your reading time is more valuable now as a young person than for a geezer like me, because of compound interest. Read enough and you may someday be as smart as I am, but you'll never have two skeletons and two hearts in one body, like a mom.

* In Japan, that unread pile gives you "tsundoku," the guilt of not reading.

How to Speed-Read Like Theodore Roosevelt

A NEW BOOK is published every thirty seconds. The median number of books an American reads per year is six. It would take fifteen thousand lifetimes to read the books published in a year, or a mere 163 lifetimes if you limited yourself to every book available on Amazon. If you want to keep up at all, you've got to take a cue from one of our greatest presidents, Theodore Roosevelt. When he was a child, Roosevelt taught himself to speed-read, and he educated himself by reading because he was too sickly to attend school. He was famous for reading three books a day, including an entire book with breakfast. Follow Roosevelt's method and you'll be following in the footsteps of the man known as "the locomotive in human pants."

1. Review the table of contents and the section headings. This will alert you to the main ideas and important through-lines.
2. Train your eyes to use your peripheral vision. You don't have to read and internally vocalize every word. Your brain can comprehend several words at once. The speediest readers read multiple words at a time.
3. Scan and skim: Sweep your eyes across the page, looking for key concepts. Jump over articles like a, an, and the.
4. Use your finger to guide your eyes along the page to avoid backtracking.

Hermann Ebbinghaus, a German psychologist, developed the idea of the "learning curve," meaning that when we first learn something, our knowledge increases exponentially, then that rate of increase gradually levels off. But he also studied the "forgetting curve." Unless you use what you've learned, you will forget it at a stunning rate. Humans forget up to 80 percent of what we learn within twenty-four hours, unless it's reinforced by using the information, reviewing it, taking notes, or sharing it with someone else. "Reading without reflection is like eating without digestion," according to the political philosopher Edmund Burke.

Your aunt Kate and I are known for having astonishing memories. We discovered an event called the USA Memory Championship and were keen to enter.* Kate and I practiced mnemonics and engaged in some sisterly trash talk about who has the better memory (it's me). How did we do? Well, both of us forgot to send in our application.

I'm more careful about remembering what I read. I take the slippery book jackets off and I write notes in the endpapers. I scribble comments in the margins. I often fall asleep reading my books and with my special left-handed ink pen, I draw all over dad's back in my sleep. I leave Robert Motherwell–like stains on the bed linen. I am passionate about retaining what I have learned.

Jack, you have the advantages of a great education. Your father and I have inspired a love of learning and instilled within you an armory of Stoic wisdom. This is your inheritance; the

* The mascot for the USA Memory Championship is a seahorse, in honor of the brain structure called the hippocampus where memories are formed. In fact, "hippocampus" literally means "seahorse" in Greek.

rest goes to the cat. As Epictetus stated, "Only the educated are free."

Your character, intelligence, and integrity can never be taken from you. You have the gift of faith and a foundation of Stoic virtues. It is my greatest wish that you continue to develop and use your gifts to fulfill your life's purpose. Michelangelo wrote that "the greatest danger for most of us is not our aim is too high and we miss it, but that it is too low and we reach it." Shoot for the moon. Shine on, my son.

Per aspera ad astra—through hardship to the stars,

Mom

Bibliomancy

Bibliomancy is a form of divination, using a randomly chosen passage from a book to answer a question or get advice or insight. The practice of using a book to tell the future is as old as books themselves. It's probably even older, as Torah scrolls are sometimes used for the purpose. The method is simple. Pick a book, often a bible or a philosophy book, but any book that has significance for you will do. Think of your question and hold it in your mind. Close your eyes and let the book fall open, then put your finger on a page. Read the word or phrase you've selected (you can open your eyes for this part) and, as the belief has it, the book will give you the answer you seek.

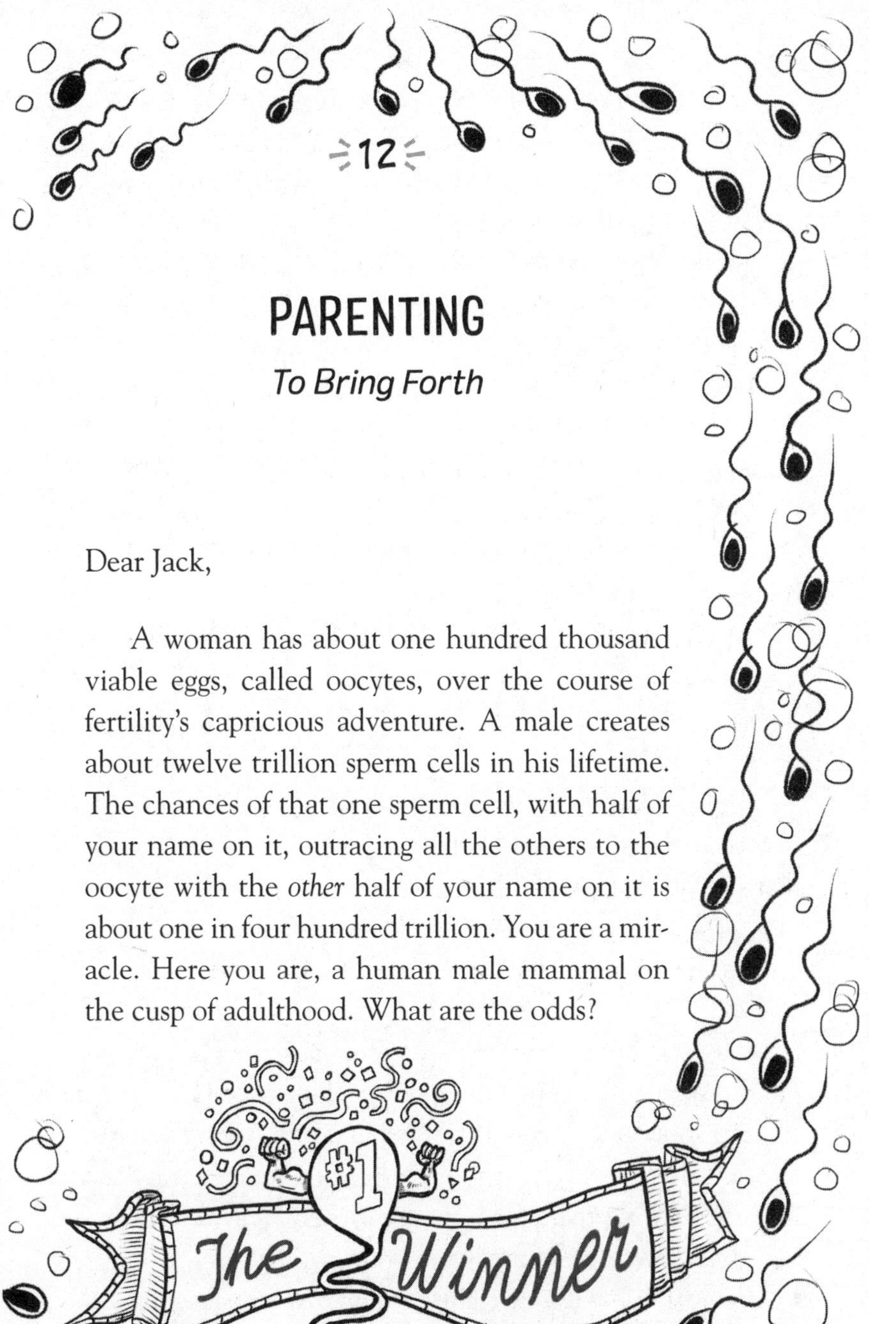

12

PARENTING

To Bring Forth

Dear Jack,

A woman has about one hundred thousand viable eggs, called oocytes, over the course of fertility's capricious adventure. A male creates about twelve trillion sperm cells in his lifetime. The chances of that one sperm cell, with half of your name on it, outracing all the others to the oocyte with the *other* half of your name on it is about one in four hundred trillion. You are a miracle. Here you are, a human male mammal on the cusp of adulthood. What are the odds?

A male sea catfish holds fertilized eggs in his mouth until they hatch in a process called "mouthbrooding." If you were a sea catfish small fry, your father's mouth would have played the part of your mother's lady bits.

Had you been born a baby mole rat, your diet would consist of your elder siblings' fecal pellets. Think about that the next time you're disappointed at getting served leftovers.

Had you been conceived as a sand tiger shark, you would have grown a razor-sharp set of embryonic teeth. Why? Why, the better to eat your womb-mates with! Devouring your unborn siblings is a practice called intrauterine cannibalism. Only one sand tiger pup is born; the strongest had all its sisters and brothers as a pre-birth snack.

At your birth, the clock started on your life. I punched into a new life as well. You created a new gig for me: being your mum. Your existence, the fact that you breathed the same air, took my breath away. Your father and I were enchanted to be your parents.

Biology doesn't determine maternity. Just as there are many ways to become a parent, there are many ways to parent. Humans have their own biological quirks, just like sea catfish, mole rats, and sand tiger sharks; we just don't eat our young. Our quirk is metamorphosis. I have one son, but I didn't parent just one kid.

I am the mum to all the different Jack the Lads, in all the various stages of your life: the spooky, jelly-necked newborn with the soft spot on the skull; the chubby, smiley baby; the daredevil toddler; the cheeky preschooler; the sporty elementary schoolboy; the near-mute preteen; the hilariously funny high schooler; and the soon-to-be young adult, your own man.

Parenting has about eighteen stages. Each stage lasts about a year. I was lousy at some and I modestly claim brilliance for others. No one is perfect at all of them. There is no twenty-five-year gold watch, no retirement.

There is no clear ending of one stage and beginning of another. The transition appears seamless, and I never got to say "bon voyage" to all the small people you were. We parent differently for every age and stage of our kid's life. I think I've hit my stride in the high school years. Parenting is a long-term learning experience, and parenting a teen is like grad school. You can cruise the easy parts, but you can't blow off the finals. I've almost earned my advanced degree, and when I graduate, you fly the coop.

In you I now have a son who towers over me, one whose mustache rivals my own. You are growing up and growing away. The role of parenting has a limited run. That's how we know we've done it right, when you matriculate to your own life. Yet no matter where you go or how old you are, your parents will always love you.

A parent's love is eternal. On April 12, 1915, Harry Elkins Widener, Harvard Class of 1907, boarded the Titanic with his parents. Harry was a bibliophile and had been traveling Europe to add to his rare book collection. When the Titanic sank three days later, Harry and his father, George, drowned in the catastrophe. Harry's mum, Eleanor Widener, was rescued. In response to the tragedy, Eleanor endowed the Harry Elkins Widener Memorial Library at Harvard as a tribute to her son and his love for books. The legend that prevails is that when Eleanor inked the deal to construct the Widener Library, the bereft, grieving mother stipulated that every student at Harvard must pass a swimming test. She wanted to spare any other mother from having to bear the same fate. In addition, it is said that ice cream, Harry's favorite dessert, is served somewhere on campus every day in his honor. The library and the legends are the enduring legacy of a mother's love for her son.

A parent's love can ignite purpose in the face of unfathomable tragedy. When Nicole Hockley's six-year-old son, Dylan, was murdered in the Sandy Hook massacre, she took action and helped found Sandy Hook Promise, an organization dedicated to preventing gun violence. Our family has supported Nicole's efforts, and we've hosted dinners and fundraisers to help keep American schools safe.

Nicole invited Joe Biden to speak at the fifth anniversary event for the organization. He addressed the room not only as a distinguished statesman but as a grieving parent. He spoke of his pain when in 1972, his wife, Neilia, and three children were in a horrific car accident. Neilia and their eighteen-month-old daughter, Naomi, were killed, and his two young sons, Beau and Hunter, were critically injured. He spoke about turning parental love into purpose. He said that in life, we need three things to guide us to our purpose: something to love, something to do, and something to look forward to. He commended the parents of the Sandy Hook Promise for taking action in the face of incomprehensible grief.

In the church attached to your primary school, there is a memorial for a passenger on the Titanic. Edith Corse Evans was one of four female first-class passengers to perish. Edith was single and had no children, and she insisted on giving up her seat in a lifeboat to a mother. You saw the stained-glass window above her monument every time you went to chapel, and the inscription in the marble that read, "Love Is Strong As Death."

I pray that nothing like this ever happens to you or to any child. But I tell you these stories to show how tragedy can never extinguish love. We should marvel at the magnitude of this love, this pragma we feel for our children.

This is what parents do. We try to protect our kids by offering a library for swimming lessons, by creating a nonprofit dedicated to sane gun laws so other kids will be safe, or just by making sure you get vaccinated. A parent's love is without end, without measure.

For most of my life, I wasn't in any hurry to have children. It was another late-in-life epiphany when I realized that I *did* want to have a wee, incontinent, cheeky human attached to me. Your father kindled this desire in my heart, but I was out of the baby-making business for most of my thirties. I was dealing with a debilitating disease called neurosarcoidosis that required major medical intervention. I was on a powerful drug that kills fast-growing cells, and it took seven years of weekly injections and long hospital stays to get my neurosarcoidosis under control. Chemotherapy shut down my fertility shop. I was fighting for my life, but once I was stable, we wanted to bring you to life.

When a woman is over age thirty-five and desires to have a kid, the proper medical term is "geriatric pregnancy," describing a would-be mother who must use a walker with tennis balls to hobble her liver-spotted, turkey necked, prune-faced, hunchbacked bag of bones to the fertility clinic. The female reproductive system's window closes with a shattering slam, and I had been through a chemical menopause twice. I pried open my window with my wizened claws and shouted out that we were going to go for it.

The process was arduous and exhausting. The pessimistic Norwegian philosopher Peter Wessel Zapfe said that "to bear children into this world is like carrying wood into a burning house." I'm an optimistic person, but we were dealing with my continual health issues and difficult fertility setbacks, and I began circling the drain of hope.

We were living in Manhattan and were scheduled to travel to Boston for one of the steps in the in vitro fertilization (IVF) process on September 12, 2001. The day before we were to depart, we witnessed the deaths of 2,977 people just a few blocks south of our apartment. I was enveloped in grief. My heart was mummified. I could not imagine bringing a new life into the world after witnessing such a cataclysmic horror, the murder of so many friends and strangers. The trauma of death erased the promise of life in my heart.

That night, I confessed to your father, "There is no way I can bring a child into this broken, catastrophically unstable world." He turned to me and said with assurance, "Our son Constantine Eleftherios Agamemnon Lambropolous will bring virtue and goodness to the world." He always knows what to say. He knew he could make me smile by calling you an elaborate old Greek name. He gave me the strength to find the faith to continue the unpredictable adventure to bring you to the world.

By the time I was healthy enough to try, I was in the bottom of the ninth inning of the childbearing game. We faced devastating losses and endured challenge after challenge. Every time an IVF cycle failed, it was a hammer to the heart. By the fourth cycle, my spirit was hanging by a thread. I was in a state of suspended misery. The space between the transfer of the embryo and the results was a time I could not speak. I felt weepy, but not a tear squeezed from my eyes. It was a kind of sad sickness. I had a medical illness that caused chronic pain and a lesion the size of a number 2 Ticonderoga pencil stabbing my brain and spinal cord, but the sick sadness of a fertility failure is a different, bereft, hollow feeling.

I knew there was a limit to how many times we could sustain an IVF cycle. I prayed for the strength to accept either outcome. I buried myself in prayer. I read the Stoic philosophers and continued my careers as a writer and TV host. I persevered in my volunteer work. In helping others, I found the strength to carry on. I got a lift as a mentor to young female scholars. I kept up my work as a grief counselor and my dedication to the residents at the Village Nursing Home. Trying to be useful when you feel useless seems to work. Agape gave me strength.

Your father and I faced almost three years of unsuccessful fertility treatments and we didn't raise a white flag. The experiences we endured forced us to grow together as we faced these difficult years. My best pal, Peg, reminded me that I was one of the luckiest people in the world. She said, "I bet that if you really want a baby, a stork will drop one off on your doorstep." I was seized with the image of an enormous stork circling over Greenwich Village, and it gave me hope. You can get hooked on hope.

We wanted to have a kid. It was as simple and as complicated as that.

The word "parent" comes from the Latin "parere," meaning to bring forth. We brought you forth into the world. My DNA commingled with your dad's and we made you through the miracle of life and a big shove from modern medicine. We made a human being. You made us parents.

Parenting greases you up for the art of love whether you thought you were ready or not. When you meet your kid, you are a parent whether you are ready or not. I've been immature for most of my existence; I kept my emotional life miniaturized like a bonsai tree arborist. Having a child was like a massive shot of Miracle-Gro. My love for you reassembled me and you rewired my motherboard.

I found that parenting is more fun than it seems. I'd say the hardest part of parenting is the kids. The second hardest is not laughing when they're being naughty.

When you were in nursery school, your dad sat me down for a serious conversation. He made the brilliant point that I was forbidden to teach you the armpit fart trick. This was non-negotiable. He insisted that you had to learn it on your own from one of your friends, and when you came home to perform it, I had to act horrified—even though witnessing you armpit fart "Take Me Out to the Ball Game" was one of my favorite musical performances of all time. Children are proof that God has a sense of humor. One of my jobs as a parent is to inspire and cultivate your sense of humor.

Sometimes parenting is like a pachinko machine: all you can do is watch the ball drop and hope you win a prize. At other times it's like a batting cage, and you go in swinging as hard as you can. Sometimes you connect, many times you whiff, and every now and then you get hit in the nuts. Wear a cup when parenting.

I've read that 94 percent of mothers feel guilt about their parenting. I think this is not helping mothers or their kids. Focus on the results, not your own feelings. "Trust yourself, you know more than you think," in the wise words of Dr. Benjamin Spock.* We learn as we go, and there is no easy way to parent. It's a lifelong adventure. Accept that making mistakes, and learning from them, is a huge part of it.

* Just as you shouldn't confuse Stoicism with stoicism, don't confuse Dr. Benjamin Spock with Mr. Spock of *Star Trek*. Dr. Spock was a renowned pediatrician and childcare expert; Mr. Spock is a half-human, half-Vulcan officer on the USS *Enterprise*. Also, remember that being a Stoic doesn't mean eschewing your emotions like Mr. Spock.

Frederick Douglass wrote, "It is easier to build strong children than to repair broken men."* The stakes are high with parenting. It's teamwork; it's passing the baton in a relay race of life lessons. We screw this up, our lives aren't worth a plug nickel. Yet there are no standard rules or operating manual. There's no one way to be a good parent, but there are a million ways to be a great one.

I don't have twelve steps or ten rules for parenting you. When things go sideways, I listen and lay down guidelines. The Stoics regarded our role as parents to be the primary teachers of our children. It is through our example and actions that we parent. We instill good values such as responsibility, kindness, and gratitude. Marcus Aurelius wrote, "When you arise in the morning, think of what a precious privilege it is to be alive, to breathe, to think, to enjoy, to love."

One of my habits for the past several decades is to write a thank-you letter every day—not an email. Handwritten. Email creates a burden of reciprocity and I'm not looking for a reply. As Henry David Thoreau expressed so beautifully, "I am grateful for what I am and have. My thanksgiving is perpetual." My goal is to thank a random person in the world every day. I cultivate gratitude in this way, and when I ask you to bring my letters to the mailbox, I'm trying to model the practice of gratitude for you.

You've grown up so fast, it feels like you slammed your foot on the accelerator and you're speeding into young adulthood. Your childhood raced by like a Formula 1 car and I have whiplash. When did I first have to look up to make eye contact?

* Frederick Douglass was the most photographed person in the nineteenth century, and he never cracked a smile. He believed that spreading the image of a serious Black man would counteract racist caricatures of happy slaves.

When did you first have to bend down to hug me like I'm some little old lady?

I know I didn't teach you everything I wanted to, not that I had a set of really lofty goals there anyway. Your father and I have tried to pass on some principles, though, and I think those will serve you better than knowing how to iron a shirt.

What your father and I have tried to do is give you wisdom to inspire and guide you. At the breakfast table, we have a strict "no technology" rule. We do allow reading from the philosophy books that seem to be on every horizontal surface of our home. Epictetus admonishes, "Be careful to leave your sons well instructed rather than rich," and you'd best take that to heart because I plan to leave the change barrel in the dining room empty.

Parenting isn't all tiny socks, cute bald heads in berets, singalongs in the car, and getting pizza after a hockey game. It's a serious undertaking. We are like Sherpas* trying to guide you up to dizzying heights in the face of a blinding storm. Marcus Aurelius and Epictetus strove to be good Stoic parents, and they have taught your father and me well. We have tried to follow the advice of Epictetus, "Don't explain your philosophy, embody it."

As the mother of a young man, it's my job to help you loosen your emotional tourniquet. Our culture teaches men to repress their emotions. Don't cry when you're sad, and don't overdo joy either. Be cool all the time. This emotional straitjacket stems in part from the confusion of small-s stoicism, which is about hiding your emotions, and big-S Stoicism, which is not about

* One of your favorite former babysitters is an actual Sherpa. She is a descendant of Tenzing Norgay, who accompanied Sir Edmund Hillary on the first ascent to the top of Mount Everest. Chechi moved to New York City from Nepal and has become a part of our roster.

burying what you feel, but understanding it. "Stoicism is about the domestication of emotions, not their elimination," in the words of the wise economist, flaneur, and Stoic writer Nassim Nicholas Taleb. If you are a Stoic teenager, you will feel your emotions and express them in a way that's comfortable. If you are stoic as a teen, your emotions will back up and overflow like the septic tank at our 250-year-old farmhouse.

Every New Year's Eve, like many families, we each make a list of what we want to accomplish in the coming twelve months. Like most people, we won't do all of it, but setting goals and pursuing them is important. We also choose a motto for the year, such as "always act on a generous impulse" or "how you do one thing is how you do everything." Our motto for this year was from Ralph Waldo Emerson: "Nothing great was ever achieved without enthusiasm."

Let your light shine bright, Jack; there is no advantage or enlightenment that comes from laying low. Run toward life. Be enthusiastic about it. Being a shower-upper is really important. Seneca wrote that "the whole future lies in uncertainty, live immediately." I think what he's talking about is not only the joy of living in the moment but moving passionately toward your goals even if the future is unknown.

My job is to teach you how to create your own life. I don't tell you how to live; I live my life and you watch me do it. Parents are the lens through which a child views the world. They are the invisible tether between the world and a child. We're the dress rehearsal where you workshop your sense of humor, your personality, and your ethics before you begin your run as an adult and the star of your own show.

When I was a teenager, I knew I wanted to be of service. My family's legacy of hosting refugees, fostering kids, caring for the old, driving the sick to chemo, or even raising a Seeing Eye puppy were acts that showed me a way of life, a framework I could carry with me.

A big part of parenting is going to be slippery for adults and kids. Parents must evolve and grow as their kid blazes through the different stages of life. We screw up, and it's important to own it. I apologize to you when I make a mistake.

I recall that you once went to a party at a friend's home for both teenagers and adults. Because you couldn't drive yet, I dropped you off, and I told you to call me when you were ready to be picked up. I was worried that adults might be drinking at the party, and so I didn't want anyone else to drive you home. I also told you your curfew was 11:00 on the dot. At 10:55, I heard you coming in . . . on time for your curfew,* but driven home by someone else. I was furious and I yelled at you. I was petrified at the thought of you in a car crash. I said this was the first time you were getting in real trouble, but it wouldn't be the last.

When you finally got an opening, you explained that you couldn't get through to me because the cell service was bad. You had the idea to find a landline, but the host was deep in a conversation and you didn't want to interrupt. You went snooping around the house for a phone but couldn't find one. You didn't want to miss your curfew, so when a friend's dad stopped in to pick up his son, you took a ride with them. You knew he hadn't been drinking because he wasn't at the party.

It's a hard thing when your son turns out to be more mature than you are. You've often told me that I eat and act like

* The word "curfew" is derived from the French "couvre-feu," meaning to cover the fire. In medieval times, a bell tolled in the evening as a signal that the open fires and hearths were to be covered before bed to prevent conflagration from unattended embers.

a middle-aged teenager. I'm happy to slouch around our house draped in a comforter, while you dress properly every day. As the world slowed down during COVID-19 and the sale of sweatpants ratcheted up, you observed of me, disapprovingly, "A pandemic is no time to let your standards slide."

A core Stoic tenet is the dichotomy of control. It teaches us to stop trying to exert control over things that are outside of our power. Parenting is a Stoic exercise. It's about letting go, accepting a progressive loss of control over your child. I focus on things I can control: my thoughts, emotions, actions, and reactions. I recognize that other people's judgment of me and my family is not important. Marcus Aurelius said, "Just do the right thing, the rest doesn't matter."* I try to model good choices and set some standards. I set fairly low bars, and your dad sets high bars, and you've kind of squeaked between.

My dad always said he was not raising homing pigeons. Now you're about to fly our coop. You're a tough varsity athlete, and I have to make sense of the fact that just yesterday I was tucking you in at night.

I never wanted to be a helicopter parent, but it was hard to be chill while you got pucks slap-shotted at your gorgeous face at a hundred miles per hour. I needed to find a way to accept it. I see how much you get out of hockey. If I was too uptight, I would drain the happiness from something that's important to you.

When you're at school, the animating spirit that radiated from your bedroom walls has left the building. I feel like my heart is an empty sock puppet. I'm jonesing and you are my

---

* Marcus Aurelius had a son named Commodus who was a sad disappointment to his old man. I recommend you watch the documentary *Gladiator* for an entertaining lesson in how not to absorb the wisdom of your elders.

monkey. I love you so much, my mind is never quite free of thinking of your well-being. When I'm home and you are away, I haunt your bedroom. There is an emptiness filling your deserted room. Your life force, your humor, the way you try to suppress your smile when you have perfected an imitation or made an observation that will soon have me weak in the knees from laughter—these are lacking. When I go in to steal a pair of socks from your bachelor's quarters, it feels like someone has pressed pause. Your velocity, valor, and vigor are absent. My job is to suck it up and get on with life.

Our relationship is eternal (whether you like it or not) and I will always be connected to you, my son. I store the indelible memories of your childhood in my four-chambered organ. You carry your parents with you as well. Wherever you are, the wisdom that I have tried to share with you will be your resource. My goal is to guide you to be a magnificent addition to the human race.

Epictetus, my Stoic exemplar, adopted a son later in life. I like to think this was a good experience for the young man, not an endless series of eyerolls at the old gasbag. Now that we are soon to be empty nesters, I have raised with your father the possibility of bringing in a helping-hands monkey to assist with the dishes, fill the hole in my heart, and pour my evening sherry. There's a spare bed for him after all. I feel that animals are themselves practical Stoics who devote their attention to things they can control. Your father, however, has not really come to a useful Stoic understanding of his emotions about my desired monkey.

A son is his mother's heart, racing away
from her on a pair of goalie skates,

Mum

13

THE IMP OF THE PERVERSE

Dear Jack,

After I graduated from college, I moved back to New York City with my best pal, Lori. We struck up an acquaintance with a pair of male best friends, Dave and Neil. Dave worked in the same office as Lori and had a crush on her. Neil and I worked together, and he had a crush on me. They are only flesh and blood.

The two of them were always pestering us to go out with them, and we did—but just for fun; we weren't interested in them that way. They had an idea that we should all go to Atlantic City for the weekend. We put them off, but Dave and Neil kept after us and finally we agreed to go. They were swell guys, and it was acknowledged that this was a friendly road trip, not a romantic double date.

All of us were broke and we stayed in a run-down hovel far from the hotels and casinos. It was off season, so it was doubly cheap.

We couldn't afford to gamble and hobnob with the high rollers, so we slummed it on the boardwalk. We found a dollar hot dog joint with sticky tables and went to town on the budget-priced red hots.

This fine hot dog dining establishment sported an arcade where you could win assorted prizes, from plastic rings with a spider on them, to Chinese finger traps, to an enormous stuffed Garfield the size of a patient on *My 600-lb Life*.

In a smudgy glass case, I spotted the greatest prize attainable through the mastery of Skee-Ball: It was a shimmering gift greater than the sixty-nine-carat diamond Richard Burton gave Elizabeth Taylor, glittering with the azure allure of the Heart of the Sea pendant from Titanic. It was a blue ribbon, the kind usually awarded for pie-eating contests. But this one was remarkable; in sparkling cursive it announced, "I'm A Classy Lady!"

I knew I had to win this for Lori. While the guys urged us to head to a bar for cheap beer, I spent my dwindling stash on game after game of Skee-Ball, piling up the tickets until I got enough to get Lori the ribbon.

She pinned it on and we sat down on a bench in the frigid February wind. Lori pulled out a cigar to celebrate her new bijou, and the cigar was immediately blown out of her fingers. She got down on her hands and knees, crawling under the tables to look for the cigar among the food wrappers swirling along the boardwalk. She looked up at me, her blue ribbon whistling in the wind, and started cracking up and said, "I'm a classy lady!"

In all the successes Lori and I have shared, we often laugh the hardest about our impulsive, poorly thought-out antics. They live forever in our decades-long friendship.

There's no chance either of us could ever escape the highlights of our former humiliating jackassery, either. I knew a guy whose side hustle was making commemorative plates, kind of like the cheesy geegaws advertised on Fox News or in the magazines you find in dentists' waiting rooms. These weren't limited editions fired in porcelain, celebrating royal weddings or presidential inaugurations. They were done in felt-tip pen on paper plates and honored your most embarrassing and regrettable moments. He would recreate the time when a coworker had too much punch* at the office holiday party at the boss's house, heaved on the boss's new pool table, and was then ushered out by the boss's elderly secretary. Also, the coworker was me. My friend got very good at drawing drunk people with X's for eyes.

I scrounged up ten dollars and commissioned this guy to do a plate of Lori, with her blue ribbon, crawling on all fours, under a picnic table, being a classy lady for all eternity. I have always been a patron of the arts.

I think we all carry these escapades within us. Only sometimes are they scrawled on a paper plate. These moments of regret live on as hard-learned lessons, but we hide these lessons from our teenage children. How can we grow old and wise without the lessons of being young and daft?

There is a theatricality about parenting that is pure baloney. It's a worse act than my performance in *Dumb and Dumber*. The image of your mom and dad as eternally upstanding citizens is nonsense. The idea that our mistakes and misfires should be buried in a vault should be buried in an even deeper vault in the middle of the New Jersey Pine Barrens.

We are not always governed by the highest, most esteemed version of ourselves. Yet parents tend to share the stories where they felt the hand of God on their shoulders, not the moments

* Punch is from the Sanskrit "panc," meaning "five." The celebratory libation was the sum of five ingredients: alcohol, sugar, lemon, water or tea, and spices.

where base human impulses took the wheel. Parents try to role-model perfectionism. They hold themselves to impossible standards and don't live up to them, then get down on themselves for falling short. Their kids learn that if they are not perfect, they have failed.

There are endless ways to parent, and they all seem to have a catchy name now. Tiger moms and panda dads, jellyfish dads and dragon moms; the offspring of this menagerie may be free-range kids. Parents can be helicopters, lawnmowers, bulldozers, or snowplows. There's a whole heavy-equipment-showroom-run-by-wild-animals assortment of parenting styles.

Your father and I have tried to create an atmosphere of mutual respect with you. We treat what you say and do seriously and ask you to do the same for us. Of course, we are not serious all the time, but when we need to be, we have a discussion, we speak, and we listen in turn. We haven't labeled our parenting style. I did try to push Stool Mom because the three of us are like the tripod stool in the library. We are steady and connected and hold each other up. You and your father rejected Stool Mom unequivocally.

Part of mutual respect is being honest about our screwups as well as our triumphs. I once crashed my mother's car, into my father's car, in the driveway. I want you to know my life is not an unbroken string of triumphs such as being crowned Miss Guinness, my reign as the Coney Island Mermaid Queen, and winning the Ernest Borgnine Look-Alike Contest.

We all make mistakes, get distracted, and become overwhelmed. We all make bad choices and mess up. It happens. The Stoics would ask themselves, "What can I learn from this?" But that doesn't mean you should give yourself permission to make mistakes or act out.

Edgar Allan Poe wrote a short story called "The Imp of the Perverse," in which the narrator identifies his urge to act recklessly as caused by a creature he calls Imp. This is a radical and primitive impulse within all humans. The Imp is the little fellow who advises you to do the wrong thing, sometimes mischievously, sometimes just for the sheer hell of it.

The Imp is related to your inner pigdog, but while the pigdog holds you back in laziness, the Imp urges you on toward mischief. Remember the time you left muddy handprints all over our freshly painted house? That was the Imp.

The Imp is a little like the devil on your shoulder, but it's more chaotic than pure evil. It's kind of like a delinquent monkey. Sometimes it grooms out the nits, sometimes it flings poop without caring who gets hit.

When you were four, I shepherded you and two of your preschool friends to a tennis lesson. We entered through the pro shop, and one of your pals darted behind the unattended counter and picked up a pot of coffee sitting on the warmer. Before I could react, he started whirling it around in circles over his head.

I was mesmerized. I knew that while the pot was in motion, centrifugal force would keep the coffee in the carafe, but if it stopped suddenly the hot liquid would go everywhere. We were surrounded by gleaming tennis whites and I envisioned brown stains everywhere, not to mention scalding injuries for everyone in range.

"I guess I'll see what happens," I thought. The kid managed to bring the pot to a stop without spilling a drop, and I gently took it from him and replaced it on the warmer. "Why did you do that?" I asked him, trying to keep a steady voice. "I have no idea," he replied. It was the Imp of the Perverse.

The Imp gets you into jams, but you can also learn from him. The Imp teaches you about what tempts you, what happens when you give into him, and how to clean up the mess afterward. You can learn how not to let the Imp control you and that by itself will make you a better person.

One of the biggest challenges in parenting is having the hard conversations. In the knot of our past mistakes, there is an opportunity to untangle your own dilemmas. Owning up to my experiences with the Imp can ease a bit of the pressure to be a perfect kid. Our greatest lessons are often learned at the worst moments from our worst mistakes, and if you are honest about them, your kid may not have to repeat them. As Warren Buffett remarked, "It's good to learn from your mistakes. It's even better to learn from other people's mistakes."

I'm not trying to be a cool mom who brags about her wild times and makes her kid think this is acceptable behavior. I have hard-won lessons you can benefit from.

I spare you some details, and some incidents will always stay locked up, but I own up to my faults and flaws and share how I took action to make them right. Sometimes you need to hear these stories. It is disrespectful and distrustful to skip over the experiences of spectacular failure. We vaccinate against catastrophic illness with a harmless bit of virus. You can build up immunity to monumental blockheadedness with a smidge of my Imp.

The Catholic Church teaches that there are "sins of omission," things we ought to have done but didn't. There are lies of omission too. What we don't say says a lot.*

Kids model what they see. If you are honest, they will be too. Own up to not being perfect, how you felt when you screwed up, and how you dealt with it. Show respect by trusting them with your mistakes.

Jack, you told me once that it is more comfortable to talk about the big stuff swimming around your brain when we are not face to face. Looking into another person's eyes can feel confrontational. We like to go on drives together and shoot the breeze while we look at the road and the world around us instead of staring at each other's faces. Parallel play is when babies play happily alongside each other; parallel chatting makes talking with a teenager more comfortable. We are shoulder to shoulder.

Sitting next to each other, facing the windshield, we've had some interesting chats. I told you about my grandfather and how he died peacefully in his sleep. I shared that I'd like to go like he did, and not screaming in terror like the passengers in his car.

Sometimes I'll make an ostensible destination, just so you and I can have time to talk about big things, like school and other future plans. It's also an environment where I feel comfortable sharing my Imp of the Perverse moments.

* Things we choose not to talk about are called "tacenda." These include the food dribbling down your great-aunt's shirt at Thanksgiving, and the miserly, cheap Pete antics of Uncle Flanders, our least favorite relative. It comes from the Latin root "taceo," meaning "to not speak."

Once I went to the general store with your father and sat in the car while he shopped. Through the store windows I could see a weaselly ex-friend. He spotted your dad and crouched behind the potato chips to avoid interacting.

I got out of the car and flattened myself like a pancake against the wall next to the door, like a two-year-old trying to be invisible. When the weasel came out, I sprang out at him and shouted, "Ooga boogity booga!" He started to fake cry and as usual launched into a litany of how he was a victim and life was unfair. I had momentary satisfaction from this, but later I realized nothing constructive had happened, for me or for the weasel. I just acted like a dope and regretted my actions. I was not at my best in that moment. My Imp got the better of me.

We just had our buddy Vinnie the Cop to visit. He's a former New Jersey State Police detective who wrote about his experiences under an alias. (Vinnie is also an alias.) When he sold a book about his experience, a dirty rat of a reporter did some digging on him and revealed his true name, which put him in great danger—he was working undercover in narcotics at the time. I love Vinnie very much, and I was infuriated that this woman revealed his identity.*

I ran into the weasel at a big beauty industry event when we were seated at the same table. She was moaning that her makeup artist over-plucked her eyebrows. She had two tiny commas above her beady eyes, which made her Frankenstein forehead look even more massive.

---

* Harvard psychologist Dan Gilbert has noted an interesting phenomenon where we can get more upset when a friend gets hurt than if we are. When an insult or harm is directed at us, our psychological coping mechanisms kick in and we can calm down, but maltreatment of our friends and loved ones can slip through our emotional defenses, so we may overreact when we jump to defend them.

I casually mentioned that I had heard that the drug bald men spray on their domes was as pure as mother's milk, and as far I knew, you could drink it. "Why don't you try rubbing a little on your forehead to grow back your brows?" She thanked me profusely, and then went on to talk about herself at great length. This woman was a handful—a handful of loose screws.

I didn't know what would happen. I figured maybe I had given her good advice. Months later, I heard that her eyebrows were still inchworm-sized, but she did grow a wispy mustache.

I'm not sure you will ever be in a comparable situation, but I hope that if you are you will not use Rogaine to get revenge. We all make mistakes. Everyone carries an Imp of the Perverse. I hope you will learn from mine how to deal with yours.

Rumspringa

Among many Amish communities there is a tradition called Rumspringa, which means "hopping around" in the Pennsylvania Dutch language. It is a period of a couple years when teenagers are freed from the strict discipline of church and family. It's a rite of passage similar to a bar or bat mitzvah, confirmation, or quinceañera, only with a lot more beer. The idea is that they have a window to choose between the simple, unworldly lives of their community and modern society. Rumspringa can be as tame as joining a singing group that includes both boys and girls, or as wild as driving a car to the big city to party with other dissolute Amish youth. Some run wild closer to home and get drunk on moonshine while herding sheep in the dark. Today's rumspringers can be found on social media, posting selfies featuring bonnets and plain dresses. The youthful folks who put on modern clothes are said to have "gone

English." At the conclusion of their wild times, they must be baptized into the Amish church or leave the simple life behind forever. Roughly 85 to 90 percent of Amish teens choose to return to their community; they learn from their Imp of the Perverse. Can a parent go on Rumspringa too, the wild kind, not the singing group kind? Asking for myself.

* * *

I know you will be pushed or dragged by your own Imp someday. You should try your best not to give in, but if you do, learn from the experience. "If you don't make mistakes, you don't make anything," as Joseph Conrad wrote. You could fill the Mariana Trench with my mistakes. I'm still learning from them.

Failure has such a negative vibe. Fear of failure keeps us from trying our best. Nobody succeeds in doing something great on the first try, whether it's flying a rocket to the moon or growing into a strong, independent young man. If you are not making mistakes, you are not trying. Reframe fear of failure as an indication of how much you want to succeed. These jitters prove that you care and highlight what is important.

Your grounding in Stoic philosophy will help you overcome missteps. In the words of Nassim Nicholas Taleb, "A Stoic is someone who transforms fear into prudence, pain into transformation, mistakes into initiation, and desire into undertaking." A Stoic can also turn the Imp into an education.

Today we were out for a drive and a chat, and we stopped off at the liquor store to buy your father a bottle of Jameson Irish whiskey for Saint Patrick's Day. Coming back to the car, I weaved across the lot staggering in circles and pretending to chug straight from the neck of the bottle. I could see you massaging your temples, as if gripped in pain. When I opened the driver's side door, you sighed, "I knew you were going to do that." I guess my Imp has become predictable. I could see you were hiding a smile, though.

Lord Byron advised, "Always laugh when you can, it's cheap medicine." This quote has become another family motto. In the case of the Imp, the numbskull antics of our own teenage years (and adult years) offer insight and an opportunity to share a laugh that will do both the parent and the kid some good.

William Fry was the father of modern gelotology, the study of laughter. He described laughter as internal jogging. Sharing a joke or cracking wise with your kid can increase your immune system and reduce blood pressure, which will be helpful when you are riding shotgun as your child learns to drive.

Laughter is a social emotion, and it increases familial bonds and feelings of closeness. When it feels like your kid is growing away from you, sharing a laugh together offers a moment of togetherness, when it feels like you are on the same team. Kids laughing at parents is as old as parents, and letting out a bit of the Imp is a good opportunity for both to let out a loud hee-haw.

As Ralph Nader said, "Your best teacher
is your last mistake,"

Mum

14

MY NAME IS KAREN AND I DO NOT WANT TO SPEAK TO YOUR MANAGER

Dear Lefty,

When we were trying to decide on your name, I made a list, for the first and only time in my life, of people I despise. It wasn't a long list, but I was able to definitively eliminate the names Slobodan, Primo, and Dave. It's a peculiar exercise, deciding what to call your baby. A possible name starts out as a word, then it prompts memories of people the parents know, and finally it becomes a part of your child.

Your name is an introduction and a greeting. It is one of the first words you speak when you meet other people, and one of the first your friends will use when they greet you. I didn't want your name to sound like I was trying to cast the male lead in an indie mumblecore movie. Your name is a blessing; your name is a wish, and your name casts a shadow. What we christen you with is a summary of your life in just a few letters.

As you are probably aware, your grandparents gave me the name Karen. I've never really connected with it. I believe my mother scraped the bottom of the barrel of monikers and Karen stuck to me like toilet paper on the heel of a shoe. My siblings were all christened with ancestral and/or saints' names. I'm the most Catholic of all the kids, but there is no Saint Karen; some believe that the name Karen is derived from Saint Catherine of Genoa, a member of the Franciscan order, who is fondly referred to as "the apostle of purgatory." There's also an apocryphal Saint Karen, patron saint of spinsters and washerwomen. I imagine her symbols are skid marks and hobo teeth.

Female names cycle in and out of fashion faster than male names. The XX chromosome names often reflect popular trends as well as race and class markers. At one point in the 1960s, Karen was the third most popular name. Why? I don't know. There weren't any Karen superheroines, no wonder dogs with the name, no disease-curing scientists or feminist writers or daredevils. It's the rainy Monday morning of names. But for some reason the name spread like a virus, or a weed, among the female children of the time.

Today, those sickly weeds have borne bitter fruit. "Karen" has become slang for an irritating, antagonistic, middle-aged woman who sports a lady mullet. She's entitled, tacky, garish, graceless—the opposite of cool. She's a font of abrasive behavior and a stock female villain who makes her children listen to KIDZ BOP.

Names fascinate us because of what they say about us, both as individuals and as part of society. Names are cultural indicators, and we associate specific characteristics with certain names. Every name represents an idea—an image or a memory of those who share your moniker. It is a signature we are wedded to, carrying it on our journey from birth to death.

I've always felt disconnected from Karen. I have divorced myself from it. This marker of identification never felt like me. Karen is a ghost. I feel like I got mislabeled. When I go to the coffee joint and they ask me for my name, I tell them it's for Jack; your name is so much more euphonious to me. A name should cast a light over you, but in my case, it feels more like the cloud you draw when we play Pictionary and the answer is "monkey fart."

There was no close relative or mentor who shared the same two hard syllables with me, the graceless KAR rubbing against the hard REN. To my ears the name is not music but the sound of two rusting tuna trawlers crashing into each other, at first quickly and with great force, and then with a long, slow grinding that tears both vessels into shipwrecks, but not the interesting kind of shipwreck. The name you're given is like a house you inhabit. I filled the houseboat SS *Karen* with dynamite and lit a match.

My rejection of my name was a part of my identity, even when I was very young. My parents didn't call me the K word. To my immediate family, I am "Cannonball," the nickname I earned from launching off the sofa and springing into amateur stuntwoman antics. One day, my best friend from primary school announced to our second-grade class that there are too many Karens and that I should be called Duff. This one stuck. I was mislabeled at birth but was luckily reborn as Duff.

Nominative determinism is the theory that a person's name can have a significant influence in determining key aspects of their character and profession. The classic example is the scientific paper on urology by Splatt and Weedon. These days, Duff is most widely known as an acronym for "designated ugly fat friend"—the less-attractive member of a clique whom the pretty girls keep around so that their beauty shines even brighter by comparison. Duff is also slang for your posterior. As a verb, to duff someone is to practice a deception or steal. A duff is a cheat. In golf, it's a swing that is so misjudged and ineffective that the club hits the ground before the ball. Something duff is inferior, and a duffer is a peddler of counterfeit goods. Duff is the decomposing leaf litter on the forest floor. It's the finger-staining dust left in the bottom of a bag of Flamin' Hot Cheetos. A woman who is "up the duff" is carrying an unplanned pregnancy. A duff is a stiff suet pudding boiled in a bag.

Only some of these apply to me. I've never golfed and never will, so my name didn't determine my course in life in that regard. Posterior—well, I have one. It is unremarkable. Did I turn out to be like the dust at the bottom of a Cheetos bag? You'll have to judge that for yourself, though I like to think I am spicy and delicious. I find "Duff" to be euphonious and I like it as a name, though when it comes to its significance, I may have exchanged the tepid frying pan of Karen for the inferno of Duff.

Nominative determinism isn't an iron law, though. You can also define your name by the way you live your life. Whether I have done a service to the name Duff is, again, something you'll have to sort out. I'm good with it. When it comes to positive cultural impact, it's a close race between me and the beer Homer Simpson guzzles.

Naming a baby is ceremonial, and choosing a name is a form of self-expression as a parent. The name we bestow signifies ethnicity, religion, social class, sports team enthusiasm, and degree of Star Wars fandom. Your given name is assigned to you at birth and your last name carries your ancestral history. Together they are an invitation to your being, the first two nouns of your origin story. Your full name accompanies you as a permanent marker, from certificate of birth to the chisel on your tombstone.

We give you the moniker we believe will suit you, but you must tailor it to fit. You add your own meaning to what we intended. You infuse your name with vigor and your own style. Your name is your nomination—it's us tossing your hat in the ring as a member of Team Lambros. It's also your first hashtag. It's a nerve-racking decision, and you were fortunate in that we don't have the last name Dickshot, nor were we fans of the first name Stinky, or Ratface. Or Karen.

At birth, you were a ten-pound miracle of physiological, neurological, and biochemical activity wrapped up in your cherubic birthday suit. Your father and I looked at you and asked, "Who are you?"

Like most new parents, your father and I labored over what to call you.* Your father's family has had a long history going back to the old country where Yiannis Lambropolous would name his son Lambros Lambropolous, and Lambros Lambropolous would name his son Yiannis (John) Lambropolous, in an endless Hellenic conga line of repetition. Your late grandfather was named, quadra-syllabically, Lambros Lambros (his father dropped the -opolous in the Aegean on the way to America).

* Actually, one person labored while the other called out possible names in a game of nominative bingo. Your father rejected Eleftherios, meaning "freedom" in Greek, as well as the nickname Lefty.

Your father is John Fortune Lambros. Son, you were on deck and the next Lambros up.

"Lambros" is a classical Greek name meaning brilliant, radiant, and luminous. It's related to the English word "lamp." In the Greek Orthodox tradition, the name is given to commemorate Easter, which is known as Lambri, or the "bright day." While it's common in Greece to use the same first name as the last name, I felt that multiple generations of Lambros J. Lambroses was enough. We would honor your Greek ancestors with your name, but we did not double up. "Necronym" is a Greek word meaning "death name," as in, named after a dead person. This is a venerable tradition in many cultures and religions, one that I respect and admire, but on the happy day of your birth I did not want to use a necronym.

Before you were born, I would dream about who you would be and what we would name you. I wanted to name you Luigi because when you say the name, the zygomaticus major muscle draws the angle of the mouth into a smile. I imagined you in your baby carriage, and as I pushed you through Washington Square Park, we'd run into our friends and they would call your name. As they pronounced "Luigi," their faces would bisect into a big smile and your squishy, impressionable baby brain would learn that you are a creature who attracts smiles like iron filings to a magnet. Your father, frowning, shot that one down.

There is a Roman proverb "Nomen est omen," meaning your name is destiny—nominative determinism, classical style. Your father's name, John, means "brilliant gift from God," which feels accurate. Our family must be sextuply blessed because we have six Johns in our extended family. We have three Jacks, and we love them best, so we named you John and call you Jack.

Jack is a derivative of John that originated in England. Jen was the original pronunciation and spelling of John. The Norman conquerors added the suffix "kin," which they used as a diminutive. Jen (John) became Jenkin (Little John), which morphed into Jakin, which is how you ended up as my little Jack. In Old Dutch, it was Jan, and the suffix indicating young child was -kee. If you were born four hundred years ago on the street where we live in Greenwich Village, you would be Jankee. When New Amsterdam became New York and English replaced Dutch, the nickname "Yankee" stayed in circulation. Centuries later it was attached to a baseball team that plays in the Bronx, on what had once been land belonging to Dutch farmer Jonas Bronck.

By the later Middle Ages, the name Jack became so common that it was the generic moniker for a male human. It was later used as a term for inanimate tools, like boot jack and tire jack. A jack-of-all-trades was that one fellow who could do anything—an all-around guy. A modern survey of British teachers revealed that they thought boys named Jack were more trouble, but also more popular.

The historical exemplar of this was Mad Jack Mytton, an English gentleman of the early 1800s. I learned of him when idly poking around the medical collections at the Stavros Niarchos Library. In the stacks I found a book titled *English Eccentrics*, with a chapter devoted to Mytton, and this guy sounded like a barrel of monkeys. He lived his life with reckless disregard for his own safety. Mytton was known to go fox hunting in the middle of the night, in winter, naked. He once rode a bear dressed in full livery into a dinner party at his manor house, just to shake things up. The guests dove out of the ballroom windows to escape the bear (and their inebriated host). Mytton was a notorious boozer, and after guzzling several bottles of the old loudmouth soup, he came down with the hiccups. He thought he'd try to scare himself out of them, so he set his clothes on fire. As he lay bandaged head to toe, suffering from extensive burns, he remarked, "Well, I don't have the hiccups anymore." I may have had him in mind when I decided to call you Jack.

Your full name, John Augustine Lambros, means "generous gift from God, luminous, radiant, bright day." Your middle name is in honor of Saint Augustine of Hippo. I was reading his book *Confessions* before you were born. He was a philosopher and theologian and incorporated principles of Stoic philosophy into religious doctrine. I loved that he was a nobleman and playboy before he became a saint. His prayer was, "Dear God, please make me good. But not quite yet." This could have been Mad Jack Mytton's prayer, too, but Mytton cashed in his chips before he reached the saintly portion of his life.

There's a belief that we view someone as lucky if their name sounds like luck and has the same number of letters as luck. Jack is considered the luckiest male name. (Lucy is perceived to be the luckiest name for a woman.) This belief is known as "associative magic." It is used to describe the linking of similar attributes with the hope that by association, good things will result. Perhaps it's no surprise that Jack is one of the most popular male names in the United States.

I don't believe that your name actually makes you lucky, not in the sense that the name Jack gives you some kind of cosmic thumb on the scales of life. I do believe that we can make our own luck. Epictetus, the philosopher whose maxims run on repeat in my heart, was born a slave. His name meant "acquired"—hardly an auspicious appellation. But as he wrote, "Progress is not achieved by luck or accident, but by working on yourself every day." Epictetus created his own luck through hard work; he won his freedom and became a renowned philosopher. Perhaps his name means acquired because he acquired his freedom? Seneca, one of my Stoic All-Stars, wrote that "luck is what happens when preparation meets opportunity." You're preparing yourself now to grasp your opportunities, and if you want to call that luck, I won't argue.

You're already the product of a staggering amount of good luck. The sperm cell that led to you outraced 249,999,999 others to the prize of the female oocyte. That's a feat of swimming more impressive than Michael Phelps's measly twenty-eight medals. What would you have been if that little fella had been tired that day and another one came in first? I thank my lucky stars that didn't happen. And what were the odds you would be born back when the universe began in the Big Bang? Thirteen billion years later, as unlikely as it seems, here you are, my fortunate son.

Most people believe that miracles are rare, but those people are not a part of our family. These naysayers would not last a day on Team Lambros. We believe that miracles happen all the time. Albert Einstein believed there are two ways to look at the world: one, as if nothing is a miracle; or two, that everything is a miracle. According to Littlewood's Law, you can expect to experience a one-in-a-million event every month. Miracles are all around us, so keep your eyes open.

You are my Lucky Jack,

Mum

A Short History of Names

Ancient Romans gave male children three names: a praenomen, which was a personal name; a family name; and a cognomen, which could be a nickname or indicate what branch of the family you were from. More names signified higher status. Women had two names. Slaves had only one name, like Epictetus.

Long names long outlasted the Romans. In the 1700s, aristocratic families gave their children multiple names, including using the mother's maiden name.

Parents often gave their babies secret middle names. The belief was that for a curse to work on someone, you needed their full name.

Today, naming conventions are less elaborate and less potentially dangerous. It's common for people to rename themselves.

You can give yourself an adult entertainment star name by combining the name of your first pet and your favorite Granny's maiden name. Mine is Stinkpot Maguire.

If you'd prefer to have a blues musician name, combine a physical infirmity with a former president's last name. Mine is Glaucoma Obama.

15

DECLINE OF THE SACRED

Dear Jack,

We love to travel, but as you know, it can be challenging. When you are packing for a trip south of the border, you may want to tuck in some Pepto Bismol for traveler tummy, also known as Montezuma's revenge. An itinerary that includes Mozambique calls for the provision of antimalaria pills. If your travels take you to the Holy Land, fold in a few extra white sheets from home. One of your fellow travelers may be afflicted, not by a microbe, but by Jerusalem syndrome.

This condition causes previously stable and sane folks to come under the delusion that they are a biblical or historical figure. They wrap themselves in hotel sheets and wander around the ancient city preaching the Gospel. A staggering 97 percent of Christians affected by Jerusalem syndrome are Protestants. The condition can strike Jews, too. You can't swing a dead cat in the Holy City without hitting someone swathed in stolen bed linen.*

* If this book doesn't sell, I have a surefire business idea: I'll embroider sheets with the message "If You See Me Wearing This Sheet as a Robe, I Am Delusional—Please Call 911" and market them to short-sheeted Jerusalem hotels.

The most popular Christian delusion for men is that they are John the Baptist. For women it's the Virgin Mary; there's a good-time-Charlie Virgin who invites people to birthday parties in Bethlehem for her son, Jesus, and there's also a Mary who cries every day at the Altar of Golgotha. For Jews, both men and women tend to dress up as the Messiah. One man became convinced that he was Samson and began bodybuilding so he would be strong enough to move the Western Wall. There are no reported cases of Jerusalem syndrome for Muslims, but a similar phenomenon has been noted among pilgrims to Mecca.

Rome syndrome is a condition that affects tourists in the Eternal City who are overcome by the beauty of so many sites steeped in history and religion. Art fans may faint in the presence of great works, just as the writer Stendhal did; there's a syndrome named after him, too. Author Kristofer Lenz speculates that because we are expected to feel moved by great art and sacred places, we would rather go into psychological distress instead of feeling nothing.

Paris syndrome is the opposite of the other syndromes. Confronted with the reality that Paris does not live up to their romanticized expectations, tourists come down with symptoms that include hallucinations, paranoia, sweating, and vomiting. The syndrome mostly affects Japanese visitors, and there's a twenty-four-hour hotline at the Japanese Embassy to report cases. Causes of the disorder include snooty, rude shop clerks, Gauloise butts on the streets, and the dawning realization that not every Parisian looks like a model.

The Streets of Paris Are Not Paved with Gold

If tourists overwhelmed by Paris syndrome had done even the slightest bit of research, they would have known that a better name for the City of Light would be the City of Dog Poop. Until the industrial era, dog doo was valuable because it was used in tanning leather, but modern methods made the ordure obsolete, and now it's left behind. Parisians are notorious for their refusal to pick up after little Fifi, and accidents caused by *merde de chien* send hundreds of people to the hospital every year. For a time, there were special minibikes equipped with vacuum cleaners called "caninnettes" toot-tooting around Paris, hoovering up

the poop. The city flushed the program in 2002 because it was simply too expensive. The problem is so bad that one French politician claimed that the city missed out on the 2012 Olympics because of the epic festival of feces. In front of our house is an antique iron device shaped a bit like a rake. The French word for this item is "decrottoir," meaning "device to scrape the dung off your shoes." These are common sights in Paris. If you find yourself in the city with your dog, don't let your companion leave a deposit like a native canine; you could get hit with a fine of up to five hundred dollars.

⁂ ⁂ ⁂

Clowns induce feelings in me that are similar to the effects of Paris syndrome. It's common to say that clowns are scary, and modern clowns are toning down the goofy makeup to put the rest of humanity more at ease.* But there is one group that still proudly paints on the pancake smiles and diamond-shaped eyes: Clowns for Christ.

These evangelical entertainers believe they can best spread God's word by using humor and silliness. There's even a Christ Clown College modeled after the Ringling Bros. and Barnum & Bailey Clown College. I assume the curriculum is rigorous and you need good SAT scores to attend. (Perhaps this can be a "reach" school for you.) Christian clowns proudly point to a long tradition of levity in ministry, dating back to the unfortunate comedic actor Philemon. His joking offended the Roman emperor Diocletian, who had Philemon tortured to death.

We visit Rome regularly to see friends, allow me to do research, take in the art and history, and enjoy our friend Rosella's Thursday night gnocchi. The Eternal City is my favorite city to visit, but I worry that someday I might be stricken by Rome syndrome, and I'll imagine myself to be some historical figure. Only instead of a Christian, I'll be Diocletian, and I'll go looking for some clowns to kill.

Murder, even if it is of a clown, is still a sin. I am a believer in the Ten Commandments. I practice my faith and decline to so much as slap a retaliatory custard pie at a clown.

I grew up across the street from Holy Rosary Church, and my faith has instilled a moral backbone. Your grandparents Nan and Pa Duffy are eucharistic ministers. They go to daily mass

* Fear of clowns is called "coulrophobia."

and bring the sacrament of communion to shut-ins. I was a daily communicant as well, and I planned my high school and then college schedules around mass.

My mother taught me that whenever I saw a religious item at a jumble sale, at a flea market, or on a blanket spread on the sidewalk on Saint Mark's Place, I should buy it. She didn't want articles of faith to be disrespected or neglected. I bought every statue, icon, menorah, dreidel, and rosary that crossed my path. Saint Isadore, the patron of the Internet; Saint Claire, the patron of television; Saint Genesius, patron of comedians (also tortured to death by Diocletian)—I bought them all. I had a complete set. It was a small strain on my wallet and a big strain on storage space in my tiny post-collegiate New York apartment.

Really Useful Patron Saints

In the Catholic Church, you get one or more patron saints. Your first saint is determined by your name, and if your first name isn't saintly (say, Brandy, Britney, Bayley, or Karen), your patron saint can be determined by your middle name. When you grow up and get a job, your occupation also comes with a Vatican-approved patron saint. Plus, there are patron saints of maladies, ethnicities, activities, cruises—you name it, Catholics have a saint for it. You can also choose a patron saint just based on who you want to pal around with in prayer. Here are a few of my favorites:

Saint Gummarus: was married to a shrew, so became the patron of difficult marriages
Saint Servatus: protector of mice and rats
Saint Cloud: patron saint of carbuncles and nail makers

Saint Mark: fly bites
Saint Cadoc: glandular disorders
Saint Bibiana: patron of the hungover
Saint Fiacre: hemorrhoids
Saint Benen: worms
Saint Sebastian: hockey
Saint Drogo: unattractive people, coffee, gravel in the urine, deafness, speech impairment, and insanity; truly a jack-of-all-trades

* * *

I once bought a larger-than-life-size baby Jesus in a crèche at a garage sale on Shelter Island. He must have been part of an outdoor display. I'd never seen such a big baby. I hope the Mary statue that delivered Him had an epidural or caesarean.

I didn't have any good place to keep Him in my apartment without charging Him rent, so He rode out the summer in the back of my El Camino. I forgot to take the one dollar price tag off of His forehead, so when I drove to the donut shop, I'd return to the car to find dollar bills under baby Jesus's arm-wrestling-champion-sized biceps. I donated the money to Our Lady of the Isle Church. I donated the El Camino as well, along with Big Baby Jesus.

For the first three decades of my life, I never missed a Sunday mass, no matter where I found myself. I was in Hollywood one December, acting in a movie called *Dumb and Dumber*. On Christmas Day, I walked from my hotel to Saint Victor Church. When it was time to give the sign of peace, the dad in front of me with his family turned to shake my hand. "Merry Christmas, Duff," Bruce Springsteen said. This was like meeting the patron saint of New Jersey. Hearing that voice say my name was a true Christmas miracle.

Church attendance is going down, and I'm not sure whether the clown ministry is reversing or accelerating the trend. Just 24 percent of the US population worships collectively in churches and temples every week. There is a decline in the sacred. I think just the act of coming together helped people maintain a connection to something greater than themselves. Religion unites us with our beliefs; in Latin, religion means "to bind together." It creates a community and ties us to our faith. It also inspires us to care for others.

When you don't have sacred time, you fill your life up with distractions and elevate them. What I see today is that the energy and thoughtfulness and care that once went into practicing a communal religion is now directed inward. Self-fulfillment becomes a sacrament. Comedian Tim Dillon remarked, "Imagine visiting this country and looking around and going, 'Well I think the problems in America are because people are doing too much for each other. . . . I wish they were doing more for themselves.'" In life, you only get about twenty-seven thousand days. Do you want to spend them on TikTok dances, filtered Instagram selfies, celebrity gossip, scrolling snarky tweets—a constant feed of mind-softening and spine-squishing entertainment?

Jean Anthelme Brillat-Savarin, the enormously perceptive food writer, remarked, "Show me what you eat and I will tell you who you are." If you consume social media junk food, it will also tell me who you are. Use your time wisely. "The price of anything is the amount of life you exchange for it," Henry David Thoreau warned. There is no spare time, down time, time off, me time—it's all your lifetime.

I don't take communion every day anymore. I still carry a rosary in my pocket, though.* I pray the Angelus at noon and six. We say grace at the table in appreciation of the food. We have faith in our lives. But as James says in the Gospel, "Faith without works is dead."

I am a Roman Catholic, your father is Greek Orthodox, and you attend Episcopal chapel at your school. You've got your bases covered. Rather than try to fit you into any one mold, we have tried to share our commitment to good works and teach you by example. This is called "living faith."

Faith is a way to interpret our lives. It is one part of the scaffolding that holds me up. Another part is love for our family and for others—people I know and people I just know exist. Stoic wisdom in its clarity and simplicity is another illuminating pillar of my life. The Stoic notion that we should be judged not by what we say but by our deeds inspires me. Living faith is interpreted by Seneca's advice: "Works not words." When I pray, I'm seeking courage to step up and guidance on how to act.

Stoicism isn't a religion, but as a philosophical doctrine, it focuses on virtue. Among its highest qualities it esteems love, forgiveness, compassion, and charity, just as Christianity does. Many Stoic ideas are reflected in Christianity; both Seneca and Saint Paul talk about the need to be content with your circumstances, whether hungry or well fed, rich or poor. In fact, there are so many similarities in Seneca's and Paul's thinking that some enterprising fourth-century fellow forged

* My favorite piece of jewelry is an antique nun's ring your father found in Paris. It's a delicate, simple gold band with a white enamel cross. If Christ had been executed in modern times, would my ring bear the image of a noose, or an etching of a guillotine? Or a microscopic hypodermic needle, or a tiny electric chair?

a correspondence between them. Early Christians like Saint Justin Martyr and Christian theologian Origen praised Epictetus and the man who taught him Stoicism, Musonius Rufus. Monastic communities used some of the ideas in the *Enchiridion* for their rules; sometimes these were attributed to Saint Paul instead.*

I have a happy-go-lucky, fly-by-the-seat-of-my-pants nature. Some people have resting brunch face. I have resting clown face; I look like I'm about to crack a smile at all times.† People assume that Stoicism means you've got a serious stick up your keister, but happiness is a very Stoic emotion. Seneca advised, "We should take a lighter view of things and bear them with an easy spirit, for it is more human to laugh than lament it." For me, Stoicism means do good, have fun, and try not to hurt anyone.

I don't have some secret knowledge that will unlock the key to a fulfilling life or an equation to harness the power within. What I do know is that being of service offers something that feels like happiness to me. I go about my day trying to string a couple of small victories together and then go for a hat trick.

My friend Donald Robertson wrote that Stoicism "entails the exercise of wisdom, kindness, and fairness in our relationships with others both individually and collectively." There is good in the world to be done, so do it. In the Catholic religion there is also the notion of a sin of omission, or how we hurt

* In the book of Acts, Paul unsuccessfully tries to convert Stoic philosophers in Athens.

† My cockeyed smirk is caused by the risorius of Santorini, a facial muscle that got me scolded in parochial school and makes me look like I'm laughing at funerals. You've inherited many things from my side of the family, but fortunately not that. The tendon tendency skipped a generation, and you are unmarred.

ourselves and others by not taking action. As Voltaire wrote, "We are all guilty of the good we do not do."

Jack, in helping others, you help yourself. This is the wisdom of the heart. It is the thoughtfulness of FaceTiming older relatives, rallying your friends to buy toys for kids at Christmas, donating the gift cards you receive for your birthday, or driving around on a hot day to hand out cold drinks to hard-working street repair crews.

You're a varsity athlete, and to maintain your peak health, you took a strength and conditioning class. You ditched the other jocks and worked out next to the chubbiest, most out-of-shape kid. Three days a week, you inspired and encouraged him. I never saw this and you never mentioned it, but one day your trainer pulled me aside to tell me you'd taken this boy under your wing. You chose to work out with him, and I admire you. These small acts are heart driven, and I am prouder of this than of your academic honors. These are the building blocks of character.

Exhibitionism seems to be a commandment these days, the immodest documentation of everything we do on social media. Marcus Aurelius wrote that "it's quite possible to be a good man without anyone realizing it." It is also possible to do a good deed without posting about it. I'm glad to know what you did, and I'm also glad you can act for good without needing to shout about it.

Life is unpredictable. A beaver can chew through your Internet connection and an autoimmune disease can leave you with chronic pain for the rest of your life. You can get jilted, win a scratch-off, or fall into a pond filled with electric eels. This is your one shot at life, so make the most of it. Live your faith, my son. In the words of Travis Durden in *Fight Club*, "This is your life, and it's ending one minute at a time."

It can seem that there are so many problems in the world that it's impossible for you to address them. Stoicism tells you the opposite: the world is filled with opportunities for you to do good. Epictetus, in *Discourses*, noted that "if you want any good, get it from yourself."

Do what's right because it's the right thing to do,
Love, *Mum*

Minced Oaths

Our ancestors had a strong aversion to blasphemy. Sometimes this was even against the law—if you used the name of God in vain, you could get sent to the pokey. In many places, profaning religion can still get you a fine, a stretch in the clink, or even executed. Naturally those were things most people desired to avoid, so to be sure they didn't run afoul of Johnny Law, your English-speaking forebears came up with what are called "minced oaths." These turns of phrase allow the speaker to express strong emotion without offending the deity or the government. Common minced oaths include:

Bloody = a contraction of "by Our Lady" (that is, Mary)
Christ on a crutch = Christ on the cross. This one is only very lightly minced.
Egad = by God
Gee whiz = Jesus Christ
Holey moley = Holy Mary
Judas priest = Jesus Christ

Land's sakes = for the Lord's sake
Suffering succotash = suffering savior

In the United States, at least, we can now say "Holy Mary!" or "suffering savior!" all we like without fear of earthly penalty, in a clear sign of the decline of the sacred. The pigeons of sacrilege have come home to roost.

* * *

16

THE STRANGEST OF PLACES

Dear Lucky,

When I reflect on my childhood, I think of the Fourth of July with my Nan Chickie at her house on the Jersey Shore. The image I carry of Chickie is her tending a speckled enamel steamer pot, big enough to poach a missionary, simmering on the top of the stove. The pot had a spigot and "CLAM" was written in script on the side, in case the smell didn't give it away. Your aunts and uncle and I would be mesmerized as Chickie and her sister, Gig, sipped clam broth out of her Royal Doulton Old Country Roses fine china cups as if it were afternoon tea with the Duchess of Chatsworth. It turns out my Proustian madeleines are Jersey Shore clams.

Every family has its own traditions, celebrations, and ecosystems. You, your father, and I are interdependent, and we flourish together. We share experiences and understand one another in a way that other people never will. We are a contained unit, a bit like a terrarium, without the slimy, cold-blooded reptiles in a cloudy tank.

When it's time to celebrate your birthdays, I always get you a Cookie Puss ice cream cake from Carvel, and I take care to compose a special message. For your last birthday, you extinguished candles on a cake that read, "Congratulations On Getting Out Of Jail." When dad and I celebrated our wedding anniversary with your father's family, I had them write "Commemorating 23 Affair-Free Years."

Birthday Candles

ARTEMIS WAS THE Greek goddess of the hunt and the moon. Each month, the ancient Greeks put a candle on a little honey cake in her honor. The cakes were round like the disc of the full moon, and the light of the candle recalled its glow. When the flame was blown out, the smoke carried prayers up to the goddess and warded off evil spirits.

The modern tradition of birthday cakes with candles seems to have begun in eighteenth-century Germany, when cakes were adorned with a candle for each year and many more besides, to indicate a long life. The candles weren't blown out but were left to burn, which must have resulted in a singed, waxy mess.

The old idea that smoke can bring prayers to heaven lives on in the modern superstition that the candles must be blown out in one breath for your birthday wish to come true. Of course, what really happens is that you're spewing germs all over; bacteria on the surface of a cake increases by as much as 1,400 percent after blowing out candles.

Carvel ice cream was founded by Tom Carvel in 1920, but it was only in 1972 that he introduced the Cookie Puss cake that now supports your annual tapers.

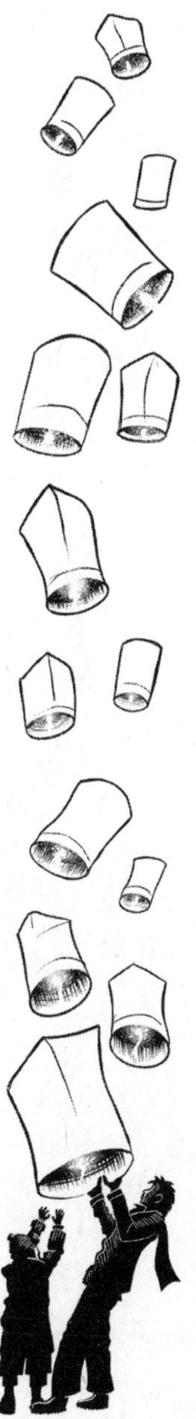

Sky lanterns are another celebratory family geegaw. These are paper lamps with a candle inside. You light the candle and they float up into the air. I send them up in winter, when we could all use a little brightness. One evening we set one aloft and the lantern glided up, took a hard right turn, and got stuck in the eaves by our bedroom. The paper caught on fire and you and your father pelted it with snowballs to put it out. This past December, after sending a flock of them up on New Year's Eve, we got a call. "This is the Litchfield Fire Department. The opera house is burning and we got a report of flaming balloons coming from your direction. Do you know anything about that?" It was your Pa Duffy, calling me from another room, yanking my chain.

Families have inside jokes and mottoes and theme songs that may make no sense to an outsider. There are specific rituals, such as saying grace before eating dinner, hiding a rubber cockroach under one another's pillows, or laying a bonfire just so. Families have traditions around types of pets. There are dog families, cat families, even donkey or weasel families. We are New York Rangers fans, but your Duffy family relatives cheer for the New Jersey Devils. The Lambros side of your family has a certain way of whistling and the Duffy family has another, but you learned from Billy's boys and are creating a new tradition.

A "familect" is a way of speaking within a family that outsiders don't get. It's a way of reinforcing bonds and reliving good memories. It is our cheeky nicknames for one another. It's our specific Lambros vocabulary. We have lots of words in our familect from when you were small. Cold weather is our "chappy" season. When you rub something between your hands you are "scrumbling." A stomachache from a bad clam is a "tummyegg." A wicked case of the "monkey squirts" can follow a tummyegg. That nervous feeling before the start of a hockey game is "jimmylegs."

When you were two, I bought several pairs of toddler-sized vintage jeans because I never liked the stretchy elastic waistbands on newer little boys' clothes. Your new old pants would have fallen down without a belt, and I found a cool, western style beaded one at the posh cashmere shop on the Litchfield Green. You wore it every day for years and when you outgrew it, I returned to the shop to get the next size up. I asked the salesperson where I could find the beaded leather belts for kids. She told me they never carry any children's apparel and I must have purchased the belt at another shop.

I knew it was somewhere in the store and that the shop assistant was mistaken. When I spotted several of them at the cash register, I was stoked to buy you another stylish belt. That is when the lovely gal who was assisting me told me they were not baby belts, they were for dogs. For years, I had dressed you in a Great Dane's collar. I guess I never noticed the brass D ring where you clip the leash. Whenever we pass the village green, I always ask whether you need a new belt, which maybe is getting a little tiresome for you now that you're sixteen.

Knockaround Clothes

In Japan, casual clothes are called "two-mile clothes," the strata of your wardrobe that you wear within two miles of your home—comfortable, scrappy, everyday attire you put on to walk the dog, mail letters, run errands, or go to the deli. These are indoor casual clothes that you wear outside the home. Two-mile clothes are now a part of fashion worldwide and were a growing trend even before the pandemic made us look like we were all on our way to the gym. Within a roughly two-mile radius, you're less likely to put on pants with a waistband and zipper. The farther you have to go, the more likely you are to put on pants that require a belt. You and your father have your own version of this trend. You are much more formal dressers than I am, and you have your "away uniforms" of sports coat, collared shirts, and belted trousers. Your home uniform can be more casual; any shirt without a collar or work-out shorts are "knockaround clothes." You didn't realize this was family slang until there was a fire at the laundromat and we had to file an insurance claim. In listing the clothes you'd lost, you included "four knockarounds," not realizing that the insurance company wouldn't understand your term for shorts and T-shirts.

* * *

Families share heroes and role models, too. We have our own Mount Olympus populated by Epictetus, Fats Waller, environmentalist Aldo Leopold, and our favorite household saint, Thérèse of Lisieux, The Little Flower. Our unanimous choice to sit on the throne of Zeus is basketball legend Bill Walton.

Walton is my all-time favorite basketball player. He won two national titles when he was in college at the University of California, Los Angeles, and two NBA titles as a pro. He was a three-time college player of the year, won the NBA Most Valuable Player award, and was MVP of the NBA Finals. His career is commemorated in the Basketball Hall of Fame.

His success was hard-earned. He suffered his first injury when he was fourteen and was hurt for most of his pro career. He had congenital structural abnormalities in his feet, and years of pounding the boards ground his size-seventeen dogs into dust. He played his heart out and his feet off. He appeared in only 44 percent of his regular season games.

By age thirty, his doctors were worried that he might never walk again. Walton has had thirty-seven orthopedic operations on his feet, which were never fully healthy. He refers to himself as the most injured athlete in history. After his playing career was over, he underwent a procedure that completely fused the bones in both ankles. The book of Job reads like *Goodnight Moon* compared to what he's endured.

Walton stuttered until he was twenty-eight, yet he now makes his living as a basketball announcer. He calls West Coast college games and it's a family tradition to stay up late with him as our living room companion. He's a scrapper, in the game and the game of life. His passion, humor, basketball smarts, and eclectic knowledge are radiant. He is the most colorful of all color commentators.

He was an artist as an athlete and now as an announcer. Some work in oil; some in watercolor. Walton paints pictures with words. Picasso had his blue period; for Bill Walton it's always the love period. His great gift is the incandescent use of the word "love." When calling basketball games, he offers lists of random things he loves as the game flows on: "I love volcanoes. I love my chair. I love my wife, Lori. I love bicycles." Yet it never seems overdone. I love this about him.

I really fell for Bill Walton when I read his book, *Back from the Dead.* Like my other all-star philosopher, Epictetus, he lives in chronic pain. He describes a moment when he was lying on the floor gripped in agony. The pain was like "a vat of scalding acid with an electric current running constantly through it. A burning, stinging, pulsating, punishing pain that you can never escape, ever." His wife, Lori, came into the room and he yelled, "Stop. Don't come any closer. You're pushing the air onto me! It's too much. STOP!!!!"

When I read those sentences, my head rocketed off my shoulders. His words exploded within me. He wrote that his pain was "worse than anything I could have ever imagined. Unrelenting, debilitating, and excruciating—the pain has destroyed me." I felt understood. I have felt that pain. I have repeated those exact words, "Stop, you are pushing air onto me," but without the shout. Instead, it was through a clenched jaw, to minimize moving any muscles in my neck.

Reading Walton's words, I saw myself. I understood. I know what it feels like to live with a meth-addled electric eel swimming up your spinal cord. It's a pain that's constant, and like Walton, I refused to let it ruin my life. Discovering his book was a cataclysmic moment, like when I first read Epictetus. I said to myself, "I get this now."

Walton noted that he lived with pain for most of his life, but pain was never his entire life. He was inspired by George

Bernard Shaw, who challenged us to become "a force of nature instead of a feverish, selfish little clod of ailments and grievances, complaining that the world will not devote itself to making you happy."

I had always thought of myself as someone who had sarcoidosis and endured chronic pain as a symptom. I learned that chronic, intractable pain is its own disorder. It is called complex regional pain syndrome (CRPS), a condition that causes extreme pain out of proportion to any trauma. (The pain of CRPS has been compared to getting a finger amputated without anesthesia.) Pain can even be caused by stimuli that aren't painful, like moving air or a strand of hair brushing against my neck.

The realization that I was dealing with sarcoidosis *and* CRPS gave me a new perspective on my health. I needed to find a new approach to my illnesses.

There are days when I am in too much pain to do anything except lie still. These days make up my life and if I complained, I would be complaining on more days than would be acceptable. If I waited until I felt good enough to start a project, I would never get anything done. I have to make an accommodation to this condition. I'm no longer a sarcoidosis patient with painful side effects; I'm a pain patient living with sarcoidosis of the central nervous system.

So much of my life has been shoving the pain down and shoving it aside. I didn't want to slow us down as a family. I didn't want to screw you up by parading my problems around the house. Your father works hard, and you have school and sports to deal with. Chronic, intractable pain can turn a sunny summer Saturday into a raw, rainy Monday morning. Life shrinks away, and I was concerned that having such a physically unwell mum would do a number on your developing brain. I was an eccedentesiast.* When your father was away on a trip or you were at school, it was a relief not to have to pretend. It can be exhausting to slap on a happy face.

Reading Bill Walton's book was like bibliotherapy for me. Seeing our family's all-star talk about the way pain nearly capsized him gave me the fortitude to be honest with you and dad. He's six-feet-eleven, a big strong former ball player, and very open about his suffering. He inspired me to try doing the same.

Read Any Good Books Lately?

THE ROYAL LIBRARY in Thebes, Egypt, bore an inscription above the door that read, "A HOUSE OF HEALING FOR THE SOUL." For the ancient Greeks, libraries were sacred places with therapeutic powers. Bibliotherapy is the modern practice of reading books with the goal of easing or even resolving emotional and physical issues. Reading relieves stress and has been shown to lower blood pressure. It increases confidence and self-esteem.

Bibliotherapy has also been proven to comfort patients with depression and insomnia, which are the evil stepsisters of chronic pain. Researchers at the University of Liverpool have shown that people suffering from chronic pain who read aloud can see improvements similar to those experienced by patients treated with other forms of therapy.

So why not read Epictetus out loud? Books give you a place to go when you are stuck in bed. Inhabiting the world of a novel and its characters makes us more empathetic.

* An eccedentesiast is someone who hides their pain behind a smile. It comes from the Latin "ecce" meaning "I present to you" and dentes, meaning "teeth."

The positive physical and psychological effects of reading may help us live longer. Or, if the book is slow, life will just feel longer. The International Federation of Biblio/Poetry Therapy offers training in the practice and several levels of certification, but you don't need a diploma to pick up a book.

* * *

We don't know anyone who has endured what Bill Walton did, but his status in our family gave me a way to connect with you. His pain and his attitude toward it helped show you and your dad what my life is like and how I deal with it. His book was an eye-opener for you, too. He's part of our familect now, a way for us to understand one another.

I do believe that reading his book helped you read me better. You are more patient with me when I have to pause in conversation to let a pain spike subside. When I have to bail and punk out of an event, you and your dad let me off the hook. I found it quite embarrassing to be the unwell, squeaky wheel. I felt guilty that I was disrupting our ecosystem and siphoning off more concern than my share. Being more open has helped you understand me, but it's also helped me deal with those complicated feelings.

Bill Walton turned his obstacles into action, and no one has more fun being himself than Bill Walton. He lives in his own gorgeous reality, unencumbered by the tyranny of a dull mind. He burns the candle and whatever other combustible at both ends.

He speaks in superlatives. With every game he calls or interview he gives, he refers to himself as the luckiest guy in the world. That resonates with me. I also consider myself the luckiest person in the world. I guess both of us can be right. It's not a competition.

Walton loves the Grateful Dead and is never seen without a tie-dye shirt. He's attended hundreds of their shows and hosts a radio program devoted to their music. He played drums with them at their famous concert at the Pyramids and has a great sense of humor about his rasping vocals. Their music is his soundtrack, and his nickname is Grateful Red. One of his favorite Grateful Dead songs is "Scarlet Begonias," which has the line, "Once in a while, you get shown the light/In the strangest of places if you look at it right." I found the light in his book.

Where will you look to find your light? In going fishing, rowing crew, playing hockey, or hanging out with your friends. All of these activities help you deal with the disappointments and stresses of daily life. I hope that you will not have to navigate the crushing aftermath of a major trauma, but I also know the world we all live in.

A difficult, painful event can leave you with post-traumatic stress disorder (PTSD). This is a condition that can produce night terrors, sleeplessness, outbursts of anger, avoiding any mention of what happened, and many other negative symptoms. We often hear about soldiers afflicted with PTSD after battle, or survivors of assault. The disorder affects people who have lived through a serious illness, injury, or catastrophic event. It can strike after the death of a relative or a pet. PTSD is a serious condition that may require the help of a professional.

"Trauma" comes from the Greek word for wound. We need to heal our wounds. Our wounds can also be a gateway, the opening for a whole new life. "If you want to find your purpose, find your wound," as Rick Warren writes.

Trauma, injury, and illness can be springboards for change. Catastrophe can awaken you to untapped strength and wisdom. It can redefine who you are and what is possible. We all hope to "return to normal" after something bad happens. We can all aspire to come back better than before, too. Trauma can be an opportunity for transformation.

Post-traumatic growth (PTG) is not a new idea; it's a new name for a practice that's present in ancient spiritual and religious traditions, in literature, and in philosophy. In Greek mythology, Achilles and Artemis experienced PTG. In comic book mythology, superhero origins include many stories of PTG. Luke Cage became invulnerable after being subjected to painful experiments. Tony Stark nearly died of his wounds before inventing the suit that made him Iron Man. Peter Parker's uncle was killed in a robbery and the tragedy motivated him to become the crime fighter Spider-Man.

Post-traumatic growth happens in real life all the time. The story of Bill Walton is more impressive because it is true. Zeno of Citium, the founder of Stoicism, also used trauma as a springboard. He lost his fortune when his ship sank but found meaning and purpose in philosophy. "Now that I've suffered a shipwreck, I'm on a good journey," he remarked.

We will all experience stress and trauma.* We all live on the edge of catastrophe. You have to be prepared to meet it and to become resilient enough to get through it. Then, you have to make something out of the aftermath. No one would have chosen to endure civil unrest, health issues, accidents, or a pandemic, but

* The Holmes-Rahe Stress Scales for adults and younger people have lists of life events and then a numerical value to score how much stress you're under. See Additional Resources.

here we are. These are the traumatic experiences that gnaw on our souls. The bone-deep, jimmylegged, monkey-squirt feelings haunt us. But the upside of PTG is the marrow-deep wisdom that fortifies your spine.

Trauma is a powerful word, one I dislike using, because it can be diminished by overuse and drained of its meaning. I heard a story on the radio by a journalist who went on a seven-day, seven-country world tour with Rihanna. This would be a joyride for other people, the trip of a lifetime for most everyone else on the planet. This journalist claimed they had PTSD after the experience. I'm not here to judge, but come on.

The truth is that trauma comes in different sizes. Any adverse life event can be included. Accident, injury, bereavement, relationship breakdown, unnatural and natural disasters, death—these are all devastating.* Trouble will find us all. It's up to us to find a way to thrive in the wake of it.

Catastrophe comes from the Greek, meaning "to overturn." Stress, trauma, injury, and illness can capsize us. They can also spin us in new and better directions. Post-traumatic growth happens when traumatic events transform the course of your life for the better. Your view of the world and what is possible can be rewired and rebuilt.

The COVID-19 pandemic was one hell of a test and we were all a bit spooked by our collective global distress. We seem to be nursing a doozy of a spiritual black eye. We've all done our best, but we need to grieve for the lives lost and the life we planned but had to divert from. They're never coming back.

* Going on a world tour with Rihanna is not devastating.

We don't get do-overs. We have to accept our fate and move ahead. We need to look to a better future for all.

Jack, I admire your optimism. As the pandemic lockdown began, people were dying. Hospitals were overrun with people desperate to breathe. All the schools were closing their campuses, businesses shut down, people were thrown out of work, food banks were swamped, and the economy was in turmoil. The flood of bad news hit us with the force of a fire hose. As we struggled to absorb what was happening, you looked me in the eye and said, "We always have hope." Hope opens the door for PTG.

As a parent who desires happiness for my beautiful lad, I understand that there will be more tough times ahead. Failure, disappointment, heartbreak, and sorrow are on deck. I am helpless to prevent it. I cannot protect you from it. I cannot block the shots that are coming. I can only prepare you with the belief that after injury there can be healing; after trauma, there can be growth.

Suffering can be transformational. I started this letter writing about the Proustian clams that brought up cherished family memories. These plucky bivalves can also teach us about growth. Clams are filter feeders. They suck in water and ocean muck, strain out the nutrients, and expel the rest. Sometimes a little bit of the muck gets stuck in the clam's body, and it is just as annoying to the clam as sand in the crotch is to you. On these occasions, the lowly clam makes like its cousin the oyster and begins to secrete a substance called nacre. The nacre builds up in layers until the clam has produced a pearl. Building something beautiful from pain is the mollusk's version of post-traumatic growth.*

* Don't expect to grow a pearl from the sand in your swimsuit.

Bill Walton's coach at UCLA, the venerable John Wooden, said, "Failure is not fatal, but failure to change might be." Admitting and inventorying your weak spots is tougher than donkey hide. PTG requires guts, the courage to get going and keep going. Nike and Marcus Aurelius urge us to just do it; the motto of PTG is, just don't give up. Our humiliations, misfortunes, and mortifications are opportunities to turn things around. It's up to you to make the most of your experiences. Use what you have been through. Failure can double as an opportunity. As Seneca said, "It's not what you endure but how you endure it."

Not everyone who endures a traumatic event will experience PTSD. You can still take that incident and use it as an opportunity to better yourself. It also doesn't take a catastrophic event to begin to look at your life, take an inventory of what truly matters, and find ways to grow. Adversity helps tighten your focus, but it's within your power to focus at any time.

Life either empties us out or fills us up. PTG fills us up—with purpose, hope, and determination. We tend to focus on the impacts of PTSD. Let's shine a light on PTG instead.

The term "provisional life" refers to the idea that one day, your suffering and problems will end. When that happens, you will be able to live the life you aspire to. When you lose ten pounds, finally get a divorce, or pay off your mortgage*—then you can do what you've always wanted to do with your life. Only then will you be happy. John Maynard Keynes, the English economist, described it this way: "He does not love his cat, but his cat's kittens; nor, in truth, the kittens, but only

* "Mortgage" comes from the Old French, meaning "death pledge." The deal is "dead" when the debt is paid or when the property is seized if the payments stop.

the kittens' kittens, and so on forward forever to the end of cat-dom."

The "provisional life" attitude leaves out the most important part, which is that when the struggle is over, it's up to you to make your life better. It is up to you to grow. Happiness and positive change don't just happen. You have to create them. You don't have to wait, either. You can begin now.

When you accept life's difficulties and live in the moment, you can achieve post-traumatic growth. You embrace the cat on your lap.

These are my pearls of wisdom. I've been treasuring up these letters for you since you were born. My idea is for you to swallow them whole, like a clam on the half shell.

Down the hatch,
Mum

17

MEMENTO MORI

Dear Jack,

The Japanese town of Hikariishi had a problem—a monkey problem. A band of our primate cousins had been raiding the crops. Yes, they had no bananas, but the bandits were making off with onions, eggplants, soybeans, and potatoes. Scarecrows and protective netting were no match for the mischievous monkeys.* Luckily, three old ladies answered the call to duty.

* Monkeyshines are endemic in many parts of the world. At the international airport in Ahmedabad, India, staffers take turns dressing in a bear costume. The furry of the day runs around next to the runway, waving arms wildly, to scare off invading monkeys.

This trio of audacious aunties dubbed themselves the Monkey Busters. Whenever the gang of simian vegetable snatchers showed up, the three "badasu sobo" (badass grandmas) rushed to the scene, apron strings flying. They fired air rifles (warning shots only) to startle and scare off the thieving, sticky-fingered monkeys. These commando crones weren't crocheting doilies; they were combating kleptomaniacal chimps.

The Monkey Busters have had success, but they remain vigilant. "I will continue to do my best for the region," one of the gutsy grandmas remarked. "It's essential for the area to continue working together as one in the future."

Marcus Aurelius wrote that "everything—a horse, a vine—is created for some duty. . . . For what task, then, were you yourself created?"

These magnificent matriarchs were created to bust monkeys. Who you gonna call? Masako Ishimura, Tatsuko Kinoshita, and Miyuki Ii.

The pensioners of the Land of the Rising Sun are a tough bunch. The 2011 earthquake and tsunami in Japan caused a disastrous meltdown at the Fukushima nuclear plant. The area was flooded with deadly radiation. Many workers fled, and the plant had difficulty finding brave people to brave the dangers.

A retired engineer, Yasuteru Yamada, a courageous and noble community leader, recruited fellow elderly experts and formed the Skilled Veterans Corps. These seasoned seniors were no spring chickens, but they sprung into action.

The gallant geriatrics were not a suicide squad. They represented the best of human nature. Millions of lives were at risk. Yamada explained, "I am seventy-two and on average I probably have thirteen to fifteen years left to live. . . . Even if I were exposed to radiation, cancer could take twenty or thirty years or longer to develop. Therefore, us older ones have less chance of getting cancer."

The cofounder of the group, Kazuo Sasaki, said, "My generation, the old generation, promoted the nuclear plants. If we don't take responsibility, who will?" She went on to say, "When we were younger, we never thought of death. But death becomes familiar as we get older. . . . This doesn't mean I want to die. But we become less afraid of death as we get older."

Gray Zen Gardens

JAPANESE PEOPLE ARE the longest lived in the world, with women attaining an average of eighty-seven years and men eighty-one. Life expectancy in Japan keeps going up, too, because of very low mortality rates from heart disease and cancer. Some attribute this to the Japanese diet, which includes fish, rice, and lots of fruits and vegetables. Just 4 percent of Japanese are obese, compared with nearly 40 percent of Americans.

The Japanese island of Okinawa has more centenarians than anywhere else in the world. Okinawans originated the practice of "hara hachi bu," which has spread to the rest of Japan. The phrase means "eat until you're 80 percent full." By eating mindfully and not stuffing themselves, they improve their digestion and maintain healthy weight. People over age sixty consume fewer than two thousand calories a day, and the elders' typical body mass index is in the svelte range of eighteen to twenty-two, compared to an overweight twenty-six to twenty-seven in the United States. Okinawans have one-fifth the rate of heart disease as Americans, one-third the rate of breast cancer, and one-fourth the rate of dementia; they spend their extra years healthy and active.

The secret to the long lives of the Japanese isn't just about physical well-being. "Ikigai" is a concept that means "reason for being." It's about staying busy and finding fulfillment in daily routine; we might call it "purpose." The Monkey Busters have found their ikigai in protecting the healthy food supply of the nation.

* * *

Jack, you are young and vital. You have your life ahead of you and I know you will be a magnificent contribution to the human race. Yet as you go through your life, keep in mind the admonition of the ancients: *memento mori*. Translated from Latin, that means "Remember that you, too, shall die."

I live with a treatable yet incurable disease. As you know, I have good jags and bad jags. During one particularly bad stint, I had the last rites of the Catholic Church said over me. I'm pleased to say they turned out to be unnecessary and I came roaring back. I highly recommend not dying to nearly everyone.

I read an interview with my namesake, Guns N' Roses bass player Duff McKagan, about his life after getting sober. He described it as "extra innings." He'd pummeled his corpus so much with drugs and drinking that he ought to have departed this mortal plane. Yet here he is, still shredding and still kicking, radiating gratitude and good vibes. I could have croaked, too (though not from addiction!), and I'm playing my heart out in extra innings.

So here I am, in my overtime, chugging my round on the house, spending my bonus dividend. I've been blessed with a great life and lousy health. My heart is overflowing with gratitude. Despite my faulty neurological system, my heart gives me the strength to seize the day.

In remembering that I shall die, I get more out of life. I'm committed to doing my best service as a volunteer, patient advocate, wife, and mum. I'm squeezing as much good and fun out of life as I can. In the phrase "memento mori," the ancients are asking us to be mindful, be aware, appreciate your talents, and rise up to your duty.

Marcus Aurelius noted, "We are all souls carrying a corpse." A Haitian proverb reminds us that we are all toting coffins under our arms and don't know it. I prefer to think we are hollow piñatas, but instead of candy we stuff ourselves with amazing experiences, great memories, and the love and laughter of every day. When the grim reaper comes, he whacks us with a stick, and these beautiful moments come flying out. This is your legacy.

Paint the Town

The brown pigment many master Renaissance painters used was called Egyptian brown, or mummy brown. It was prized for the way the pigment would mix with other colors to create a lifelike flesh tone because it was made of flesh. Mummy brown was made of ground-up mummies.

In the sixteenth century, mummies plundered from Egyptian tombs were shipped in bulk to Europe, where they were pulverized and used in medicinal compounds as well as paint pigments. Medicinal mummy powder was applied topically or mixed into drinks as a health aid. By the seventeenth century, mummy-based medicines were one of the most common compounds in apothecary shops, used to treat bruises, epilepsy, headaches, stomachaches, measles, joint and bone aches, dysentery, and diarrhea. In the sixteenth and seventeenth centuries, going to the druggist would have turned you into a cannibal.

The rise of modern medicine ended the use of medicinal mummy powder, but it lasted far longer in the arts. The paint supplier Roberson's of London stocked the pigment until they ran out of mummies in 1964.

Summum is a present-day mummification company that combines modern chemistry with ancient techniques so you can enter the afterlife like a king, an eviscerated, desiccated king.* Hopefully you won't be robbed from your grave and turned into a tube of paint, unless that's your goal.

* * *

We all have dramatic fantasies of our own deaths, in which we're trampled by bulls in Pamplona, die a hero in battle, or give our lives while rescuing orphaned kittens from a flood. The World Health Organization has counted more than eight thousand ways to die. Congratulations! Today you have avoided all of them, and they are mostly ignominious ways to go.

You haven't been impaled by a swordfish, brained by a coconut, or crushed under a falling pile of coffins at your mortuary business. You didn't eat yourself to death like King Adolf Frederick of Sweden, and you didn't drink a lethal amount of carrot juice, either. You didn't put an industrial firework on your forehead and light the fuse. You didn't die of laughter like the Stoic philosopher Chrysippus. You didn't get a fatal shot to the balls

* In 1974, when the mummy of Ramses II was on a world tour, he was issued an Egyptian passport, which declared that his occupation was "King—deceased."

by a tennis ball at the US Open, like lineman Dirk Wertheim. You didn't read a premature obituary for yourself and suffer a fatal stroke like the Jamaican political activist Marcus Garvey.

Alfred Nobel also opened the newspaper one morning to read his own obituary. It was actually his brother Ludwig who had shuffled off this mortal coil, but the mistaken news item was about him. The article condemned Alfred for his invention of military explosives. "The Merchant of Death Is Dead," ran the headline. "Dr. Alfred Nobel, who became rich by finding ways to kill more people faster than ever before, died yesterday."* Alfred was stricken, but not with a fatal loss of oxygen to the brain.† He was struck by remorse. He didn't want warmongering to be his legacy. The reminder of his mortality spurred him to do something good for humankind, and he created the Nobel Peace Prize to celebrate the best of our species.

Our lives are an exclusive, one-time-only deal. Keep in mind that what you do today is part of your legacy. Memento mori is a clarifying and hopefully inspirational reminder to think carefully about how you want to live your life. Memento mori rattles your cage and wakes you up to your promise. How do you want to be remembered?

I don't see it as a worrying, macabre motto. I hope it will be a motivational kick in the pants. It can be the fuse you light to set off the Safety Powder pyrotechnics of your purpose. Memento mori is a call to action. This is why you need a philosophy for living, so you don't die pissing your pants with regret.

---

* Nobel wanted to call one of his most lethal explosives "Nobel's Safety Powder." He settled on the name "dynamite" instead, from the Greek word for "power."

† A stroke is so named because it was once believed that sufferers had literally been struck by the hand of God.

Birth and death are the easy parts. It's the living that will kill you.

You don't have to wait until you're on the greased chute to death's trapdoor to live. Memento mori, and live now. The gallant coffin dodgers in Japan are the living embodiment of memento mori. They are mindful of their years but also mindful of their duty and how they can do good. This is their legacy. As the old saying goes, the meaning of life is found in old men planting trees in whose shade they will never sit.

The fuse of our lives was ignited the day we entered the world. Time is passing, and, as Seneca wrote, "time belongs to death." I've been around a lot of death, as a patient advocate, certified hospital chaplain, recreational therapist at a nursing home, and grief counselor. I've scraped the bottom of the barrel of life with my illness. I embrace the gift of life and the magnitude of the memento mori motto.

I don't go as far as the ancient Egyptians, though. The Greek philosopher Plutarch recorded that in Egypt, during raucous merrymaking, the celebrants would bring out a human skeleton. This was a reminder that life is short, so live it up. I truly hope that the New York Rangers do not revive this tradition the next time they win the Stanley Cup.

The complement to memento mori is "memento vivere": "remember to live."

To live and to love,

Your old ma

Telephone of the Wind

In the coastal Japanese town of Otsuchi, seventy-year-old garden designer Itaru Sasaki created an installation to help himself cope with the loss of his beloved cousin. Sasaki built a classic English phone box, painted it white, and put it in his garden. The phone was not connected to anything, but Sasaki could go into it and speak to his cousin. He felt that the confined space was helpful to him as he grieved for his relative.

"My thoughts couldn't be relayed on a regular phone line. I want them to be carried on the wind," he explained. The project was almost finished when a devastating earthquake and tsunami struck Japan in 2011. Thousands of Japanese lost family members and cherished friends. The grief was overwhelming. When word spread about Sasaki's "Phone of the Wind," people flocked to his garden to share a moment with the departed.

Bereft people went in to speak their messages for the dead. Their words were carried away on the breeze. What had begun as a private memorial became a community resource. People who have used the phone describe experiences of laughter, tears, regret, pain of loss, and requests for strength to carry on. One woman said of a conversation with her late son, "I can't hear him; it's just me talking. But he heard me, so I can keep living."

—INTERLUDE—

Things to Do When You're Dead

After working as a grief counselor for people affected by 9/11 and mourning the death of a close family member, I was moved to become a hospital chaplain for people with serious illnesses. I took a year-long course in contemplative care at the New York Zen Center. My teachers, the Buddhist monks Chodo and Koshin, gave us the assignment of planning our own funerals. Dying is one of the assignments of life. We planned everything from what we wanted our mortal remains to wear, to who we'd invite, to what kind of casket—the works.

I want a novelty Halloween recording of spooky sound effects, normally used to scare trick-or-treaters, to greet my mourners. During the service, I'll have the song "That's Life" by Sinatra on a continuous loop. Janis Joplin left $2,500 in her will for her friends to "have a ball after I'm gone," and I hope my meager estate will fund a party at least that grand. I have a producer pal who will ensure that my cremains are mixed together with explosives, so I will be a part of the Karen Duffy Lambros memorial fireworks show, titled "Going Out with a Bang." I've budgeted for a frozen margarita machine *and* a cotton candy machine. You only die once.

P. T. Barnum remarked that the press only said nice things about people after they died. The *New York Sun* newspaper obliged him by running a glowing obituary on the front page with the headline, "Great and Only Barnum—He wanted to read his obituary—Here it is." Barnum died in his sleep a few weeks later, much comforted, I imagine. I do think it is a missed opportunity to wait until someone is worm food to show an outpouring of gratitude.

Someday, every one of us will be just a memory. Don't you want to be a good one? J. M. Barrie is fondly remembered as the author of *Peter Pan*, and Bob Marley was the groundbreaking reggae master who introduced millions of college students to the word "spliff." Dorothy Parker was the acid-tongued satirist and ringleader of the group of New York writers and artists known as the Algonquin Round Table. These people were not content to leave just a creative legacy. J. M. Barrie donated all the royalties from his book to the Great Ormond Street Hospital. Bob Marley left his songwriter royalties for "No Woman No Cry" to Vincent Ford, who ran a soup kitchen in Trenchtown, a ghetto in Kingston, Jamaica. As a youth, Marley often went to bed hungry. His bequest made certain that the soup kitchen would always feed the poor. Dorothy Parker never met Rev. Martin Luther King Jr., but she greatly admired him. She left her estate to him and provided that upon his death, which came all too soon, the money would go to the National Association for the Advancement of Colored People (NAACP). Jonas Salk invented the polio vaccine, but he didn't patent it, though he could have made millions. "Could you patent the sun?" he asked. "Our greatest responsibility is to be good ancestors." We remember and honor these people for the good they did, but none of them made their charitable bequests for the publicity.

Most of us won't enter the history books for writing a beloved children's book or creating the greatest show on Earth, or for synthesizing a vaccine against a crippling disease. What we leave behind will be the small things we did, acts of kindness and love. The people we touch will be our legacy, and that's more important than great achievements or grand gestures.

But if that isn't enough for you, there are still many ways you can leave a lasting impression after you lie down for the great dirt nap. Of course, you won't be around to enjoy them, but perhaps the knowledge of what's to come will be a comfort in your last moments. As Rilke wrote, "Death is our friend."

It's best to plan well ahead, so I have compiled a guide to all the ways you can go in style:

DOWN ON THE FARM

At the University of Tennessee Anthropological Research facility, scientists will dump your body in the woods on campus. By studying human decomposition, researchers provide police crime scene investigation units with valuable information they use to solve crimes.

LAST GASP

Henry Ford was present at the deathbed of his idol, Thomas Edison, and captured Edison's last breath in a jar. This is an inexpensive way to remember a loved one, but don't put the jar too close or you'll hasten the arrival of the very last breath.

TATTOO YOU

Another way to leave a lasting impression is to have yourself transformed into tattoo pigment. Mark and Lisa Richmond, the owners of a tattoo parlor, mixed the cremated remains of their beloved son with ink. The ink was used to create a seven-inch memorial portrait on Mark's chest.

SHINE ON, YOU CRAZY DIAMOND

Life Gem creates diamonds by extracting the carbon from your loved one's cremains. The carbon is processed in industrial presses at extremely high temperatures to produce a certified high-quality gemstone. If you'd rather not fork over your entire body, they can use a lock of your hair. Life Gem also has a service for pets, so instead of your dog's hair sticking to the back of your sweater, you can pin the entire dog to your collar.

HAIR TODAY

If your family and friends are game, you can revive the popular Victorian-era tradition of mourning jewelry. The hair of the deceased was braided into intricate patterns and worn as necklaces, lockets, and other adornments to commemorate the loss of a loved one. For this one, grow your hair out before you die.

VINYL ISN'T DEAD, BUT YOU ARE

Vinyly is a company that will form your cremated ashes into a vinyl record. Their tag line is "Pressed for Time."

SLEEP WITH THE FISHES

Ocean lovers can have their cremains mixed into an artificial marine habitat by Eternal Reef.

GET LOADED!

. . . Into shotgun shells, anyway. Holy Smoke will make custom ammo filled with your remains. Your loved ones will have a blast. Heavy metal legend Lemmy Kilmister of Motorhead chose to leave golden bullets filled with his ashes to his closest friends. They are engraved with his name and meant to be treasured, not fired.

LIGHT UP THE NIGHT!

If you'd rather go out in a non-lethal blaze of glory, there are multiple companies that will mix your ashes with gunpowder and other chemicals to create a post-mortem fireworks display. This is perfect for people who are looking for a grand finale.

FLY ME TO THE MOON

The company Celestis will rocket a portion of your remains into space—for a price. Earth orbit is most affordable, lunar orbit is mid-priced, and deep space is the most expensive. The remains of LSD pioneer Timothy Leary and *Star Trek* creator Gene Roddenberry went up on the same flight.

I'M GOING TO DISNEYLAND!

Disneyland isn't just a graveyard for your wallet and dignity—it's a final resting place for Disney superfans. Although it is officially discouraged, family members have scattered the ashes of loved ones on their favorite rides and attractions. Pirates of the Caribbean and the Haunted Mansion are magnets for remains, if you're wondering why your seat is dusty. When employees discover cremains in the park, they call a "Code HEPA."

GRANDPA'S ON THE ROOF

Edward Headrick was a manager at the Wham-O company, which manufactures Frisbees, and claimed to be the inventor of Frisbee golf. He requested that after his death, his ashes be mixed into a batch of plastic and made into a Frisbee. He told his son he wanted to "end up as a Frisbee that spends eternity on someone's roof."

DEATH BY CHOCOLATE

Swedish candy salesman Roland Ohisson's will decreed that he be buried in a chocolate coffin. I like to imagine he is truly in the sweet hereafter.

TO A CRISP

The designer of the Pringles potato chip can, Frederic Baur, had his cremated remains interred in one of the iconic canisters. Sixteenth-century naturalist Thomas Moffett remarked, "We are digging our graves with our teeth"; he never imagined that one day we could be buried with snack food.

SPIRIT IN THE SKY

Sky burial is an ancient ritual in which the corpse of the deceased is placed on a rocky cliff to be picked clean by vultures. It is popular in Tibet, where the earth is frozen and it's impossible to dig graves. In the United States, you can donate your body to the Freeman Ranch Body Farm research facility in Texas, where American vultures will feast on you.

PENCIL ME IN

Artist Nadine Jarvis creates objects using cremains, and she has used them to make pencils for writing and drawing. One human body will make about 240 pencils. They are packed in a wooden box with a built-in sharpener so the shavings will have an eternal resting place of their own rather than being tossed in a trash bin.

SUITS YOU

The Infinity Suit is a cotton getup to wrap your deceased body in. The material contains mushroom spores, which will blossom into fungus that is nourished by your mortal remains. The mushrooms neutralize toxins and heavy metals in your body and enrich the soil. Actor Luke Perry was buried in one. His daughter Sophie remarked that when he discovered the Infinity Suit (while he was still alive), "he was more excited by this than I have ever seen him."

PUSH UP MORE THAN DAISIES

Several companies sell biodegradable urns that can be buried in the ground. Your calcium-rich cremated remains are used to nurture a tree sapling in your memory.

EXHIBITIONIST FOR ETERNITY

The process of plastination replaces organs and tissues with plastic, essentially turning your dead body into a life-size action figure. There are multiple touring exhibits of human bodies preserved in this way, theoretically for educational purposes.

ICED

If cremation gives you the creeps, you can go against the tide and freeze your corpse instead. The body is immersed into extremely cold liquid nitrogen, where it freezes so solid it can be pulverized into dust.

GOING, GOING, GONE

In Yankee Stadium, there's a place called Monument Park that honors great Yankees of the past. Many baseball fans illegally scattered the ashes of Grandpa Superfan among plaques honoring Babe Ruth, Yogi Berra, and Billy Martin. When the Yankees built a new stadium, the team allowed people to dig up a few spoonfuls of ash-laden dirt from the original Monument Park before it was demolished.

DANCING ON YOUR GRAVE

For some Chinese people, respect for the dead is measured in the size of the crowd at the funeral. To ensure a good attendance, some families hire mobile strip clubs to lure mourners along for the funeral procession. Many people believe that rain at a funeral is a good omen; perhaps making it rain is good luck, too.

LIFTING THE SPIRITS

Not all funerary dancers remove their clothes. In Ghana, you can pay "coffin dancers" to perform elaborate acrobatic routines while carrying your casket to its final resting place. The dancers celebrate the life of the deceased and bring joy to a solemn occasion. They've never dropped a body yet.

DIY DOA

In Ghana, the deceased are oft interred in elaborately carved personalized coffins that represent what the person did in life; for example, an enormous microphone for a singer. In North America, elderly people are joining "coffin clubs," where they decorate their future sarcophagi in their own unique style.

HEAD CASE

Cremation Solutions will create an urn for your cremains that is modeled on your head, so you can stare down from the mantel at your family for as long as they live. Or you can have the urn made in the shape of a famous person, like Marcus Aurelius, or Teddy Roosevelt, or Peg Leg Bates.

FAIRWAY TO HEAVEN

An urn shaped like a golf ball can contain the remains of the beloved duffer in your life. Unfortunately, you don't get a mulligan on this round, but your dearly departed will have the best lie of their existence.

~

18

THE FOURTH TRIMESTER

Dear Jack,

It is an inexhaustible miracle that the English alphabet has just twenty-six measly letters. We can move them around and rejigger them into delightful words like gravedigger, woodpecker, or chimp. By changing just a few of them you can transform the whooping cough into a whooping crane. The word "kiss" is an onomatopoeia, a word that conveys a sound. We can manipulate these letters to express this as "smack," "mwah," or "smooch."* You can arrange tens of thousands of them to create a brilliant novel like *The Razor's Edge*, or line them up and write an epistolary book of love letters to life.

This stingy allotment of symbols can be positioned on a page in a way that calibrates the chemicals in your brain and regulates your mood. Groucho Marx's autobiography will make your brain squirt out dopamine to make you happy, *One Flew over the Cuckoo's Nest* will get the oxytocin pumping to make you empathetic, and *Old Yeller* gets cortisol leaking to make you sad.

* In Greek, it's "mats-muts."

I have used these paltry twenty-six shapes to compose letters to you about friendship, love, illness, happiness, courage, goals, resilience when you don't hit the goals, and how to overcome obstacles. They all have one message: I love you, I loved the idea of you, I loved the baby you, I love the you you, and I will love the adult you beyond measure. Jack ad infinitum. It has been more fun than I ever could have imagined to be the mother of all Jacks.

Your first dwelling was a nine-month sublet in the womb, three trimesters in utero. Your body grew from a single cell into a fully formed human. When that lease was up, you were evicted, literally kicking and screaming. Now you live in the world, which is your forever home. You will continue to change and develop both physically and mentally until you get evicted again, hopefully not kicking and screaming. This period in between birth and death, this is your fourth trimester.

The first three trimesters were shaped by the genes your father and I gave you. Your fourth trimester is propelled by the wisdom we've tried to share with you. That's what I've written down in this book.

Words are vessels. They hold love, wisdom, faith, and hope. They are more powerful than grenades. They are transcendent. They inspire us to see, hear, and feel, and they dig into our hearts and minds.

"Finifugal" is a word that means a fear of endings. When I was in training to become a hospital chaplain, the Zen Buddhist priests who taught me drilled in the admonition to observe how we end things. Endings are important. We should pay attention to how we finish things. This idea resonated with me because I tend to say goodbye with all the care and deliberation of a person with her hair on fire.

Seneca said, "Every new beginning comes from some other beginning's end." I must bear this in mind as you approach the age of majority. You're at the end of your childhood beginning, and beginning something new: adulthood. I must embrace and celebrate that beginning and not dwell on the end of my time as your guardian. You are simply continuing your fourth trimester.

I must also start something new. My time as a parent to a child is at an end, I must become a parent to a man. I am also at the end of this book and on to the next adventure. I've always wanted to raise monkey jockeys and their canine mounts to compete in the Banana Derby.

All right, now get out of here, you,

Mum

19

A LETTER FROM JACK

Dear Mom,

You told me that in New York City we are never more than six feet from a rat. In our house we are never more than six feet from a book. I was raised by a pair of book lovers and parents with curious and colorful minds.

One morning we were eating French toast in the dining room and I asked why the walls were green. You told me that in the Middle Ages, green paint was expensive and represented wealth. It became a tradition that public rooms in private homes were painted with green pigment.

At our home rink in NYC, the New York University hockey team practices wearing their purple jerseys. They are called the Violets. This led you to a loooong story about the history of the color purple. The word "purple" comes from the Latin "purpura," which is the name of a dye made in ancient Greece from the mucus of a sea snail. It was very rare and so expensive that only kings, generals, and politicians wore it.

When we visit the Wallace Collection of art, I like to take in one of my favorite paintings, *The Laughing Cavalier* by Frans

Hals. You explained that the skin tones were so realistic because it was probably painted with a pigment made from human flesh. In the 1600s, Europeans would import Egyptian mummies and grind them up to create a special paint called mummy brown.

We went on a walk the other day and I spotted a great blue heron at the edge of our pond. It reminded me of the storks we see when we visit Nan and Pa in Florida. You told me about the Lex Ciconaria, the Stork Law of ancient Rome. Romans were so impressed by the way that young storks took care of older birds that the Senate passed a law requiring young people to take care of their old parents. The adult children of the storks use their wings as a crutch for their elders. They feed the elder birds worms, small fish, and frogs. I'll do my best to live in accordance with this law.

When you started writing this book, you asked for my permission to use either my nickname or my real name. I asked that you use my real name. You told me the story of A. A. Milne's Winnie the Pooh and the real Christopher Robin. Milne Sr. based the character on his young son and his collection of nursery toys. At school, Christopher Robin Milne had to contend with jealous classmates who bullied and teased him. He took boxing lessons because of all the fights he got into. When he was an adult, Milne said, "It seemed to me almost that my father had got to where he was by climbing upon my infant shoulders, that he had filched from me my good name and had left me with the empty fame of being his son."

You told me that you wanted to write a book of letters addressed to me and about living a great life along the principles of Stoic philosophy. You promised you wouldn't filch my good name.

I was okay with it. There are a lot of bad mothers in the media, and they come in two unpleasant varieties: the naggy battle ax or the overindulgent hype mom without boundaries. In books, moms don't fare better. Wendy Torrance in *The Shining* could have done a lot more to protect her son, Danny, from evil ghosts. Remember little Pammy in *The Great Gatsby*? Neither did her mother, Daisy Buchanan. You are a much better literary mom.

I'm extremely proud of you, and I am grateful for everything I have learned from you and the Stoics.

You and dad have taught me well. You don't have to worry. I'm ready for my next adventure.

I know you are feeling jittery about me going off to college soon, but please remember the words you taught me from Epictetus: "Make the best use of what is in your power and take the rest as it happens."

You and dad gave me life, and now what I do with it is up to me.

You have been like a mother to me,

Jack

P.S. Dad, you are now the man of the house.

Appendix

The Appendix

THE ANATOMICAL APPENDIX SITS IN YOUR BREAD-box, just above your giblets. The medical adjective for it is "vermiform," meaning "worm-shaped"; it's not a very imaginative name if you ask me, because there are plenty of slimy bits in our innards that seem pretty wormy.

The function of this comma-shaped organ confounds our medical brothers and sisters. One medical camp plants its flag on the notion that the appendix acts as a warehouse of digestive bacteria to reboot your gut after a bout of explosive diarrhea. Other experts believe that the appendix is redundant, a useless leftover from our evolutionary past. Humans have many spare parts, such as the coccyx, or tailbone; wisdom teeth; and extra male nipples like Harry Styles has.

Your appendix remains overlooked and unremarked on until it ruptures and nearly kills you. Then it gets your attention. I have included an appendix to this book, but it poses no threat to your life. It is not a spare part, either. I believe it is informative, enhances the main subject matter of the book, and will bring light to your day and a spring to your step.

Legs are not vestigial and most of us use them daily for walking, dancing, ass kicking, and other miscellaneous purposes too numerous to mention. Half of your body is legs, and one-quarter of your bones are in your feet. These are crucial repositories of vitality.

Not everyone has two legs. Some have one, or none, or two half legs. Those of us with one leg only are sometimes called "monopeds," or "unijambistes" in French. Despite missing these workhorses, our legless sistren and brethren live full and accomplished lives. Let's give an interior cheer for these exemplars, and salute the adventurous, resilient heroes who never lost a step along their journey to this Hall of Fame.

- Peter Freuchen: Danish explorer Freuchen got frostbite in his leg. It had to be amputated and thereafter he used a peg leg, but it didn't stop him from fighting Nazis.
- Virginia Hall: Shot her leg off in a hunting accident, then became the top Allied spy in World War II.
- Santa Anna: The famed Mexican general lost his leg fighting the French. The limb was buried with full military honors and Santa Anna soldiered on with a wooden leg until 1847, when he was surprised during lunch by the United States Army and did a runner without his appendage. The prosthesis now resides in the Illinois State Military Museum.
- Peter Stuyvesant: The last governor of the Dutch colony in North America had lost his leg in battle but surrendered Manhattan to the British in 1664 without firing a shot.

His name lives on in landmarks like Stuyvesant Town and Stuyvesant High School, but I prefer to remember him by his nickname in life, "Peg Leg Pete." Every time we cross the Henry Hudson Bridge into the Bronx, I nod in admiration to the statue of Peter Stuyvesant that towers over the skyline.

- Peg Leg Bates: Young Clayton Bates was dancing on the streets to make a little extra change at the tender age of five. After Clayton lost his leg in a cotton gin accident, his uncle made him a wooden leg. He taught himself to tap dance and became an international sensation who performed for the king and queen of England—twice. We also admire him for his commitment to civil rights.
- Crip Heard: Amazingly, there was *another* one-legged tap dancer entertaining America in the 1940s and 1950s. Henry Heard lost a leg and an arm in a car accident and gained the unfortunate nickname "Crip." He was unable to use an artificial leg, so he danced with the aid of a crutch. After retirement from the stage, he worked for the Chicago Bureau of Sanitation and was a tireless advocate for disabled people.
- Earl of Uxbridge: The earl was in charge of the British cavalry at the titanic Battle of Waterloo. Toward the end of the day, he was seated on his horse next to Lord Wellington, commander of the entire army. A French cannonball ripped through Uxbridge, and he exclaimed, "By God, sir, I've lost my leg!" Wellington replied, "By God, sir, so you have!" The mangled leg was later displayed in the village of Waterloo as a memento and tourist magnet.

Additional Resources

The Holmes and Rahe Stress Scales

STRESS, LIKE PAIN, IS DIFFICULT TO DESCRIBE. As Supreme Court Justice Potter Stewart said about pornography, "I know it when I see it." Psychologist Richard S. Lazarus defined stress as "a condition or feeling experienced when a person perceives that demands exceed the personal or social resources the individual is able to mobilize." We feel stressed when we feel like things are out of our control.

Dr. Thomas Holmes and Dr. Richard Rahe evaluated more than five thousand patients to determine whether life stresses caused an increased chance of illnesses such as depression, anxiety, diabetes, gastrointestinal problems, heightened suffering from pain, and even heart problems. That might seem obvious, but they wanted to do a scientific study. They did find a correlation, and they developed a rating scale to help determine whether an individual is at increased risk of getting sick.

The Holmes and Rahe Stress Test is a self-exam to help you identify the stresses in your life, assess how much total stress you're experiencing, and understand how stress might affect you. Go through the list below and give yourself points for every one of these events that has occurred in the past year. If you broke up with your girlfriend twelve months and one day ago, don't count it! The higher the total score, the higher the possibility of becoming ill.

I find the test useful as a way of taking inventory and reminding myself of all that's happened to me in the past year. Everybody is different, and not everything on the list will affect everyone the same way.

It's been a stressful few years (although aren't they always stressful?). The Holmes and Rahe test can help you get a handle on just how high a stress load you're carrying and consider what to do about it. It's a prompt to evaluate your life and, if necessary, make changes.

You will always have stress. No life is lived in perfect balance, but self-awareness can help you navigate the stress. Health and wellness isn't a perfect, unchanging state, it's a process of action. Stress and illness aren't signs that you're screwing up, goofing off, or doing it wrong. They just mean you're moving through life.

Stoicism is a philosophy that inspires you to take action, whether on your own or with a wise and trusted helper. The Holmes and Rahe test is a reminder that you can always act to improve your life. You can try to change the situations that stress you out. You can try proven stress-relievers like meditation and exercise. You can also consult with a doctor if you have health concerns and a therapist, counselor, priest, rabbi, imam, or philosopher for advice. Marcus Aurelius wrote, "Today I escaped anxiety. Or no, I discarded it, because it was within me, in my own perceptions—not outside." It may not be easy to discard stress, but you have the power to do it.

Answer the questions below and add up the points next to each answer. One hundred fifty points or fewer means a relatively low amount of life change and a low susceptibility to stress-induced health problems. One hundred fifty to three hundred points implies about a 50 percent chance of a major stress-induced health problem in the next two years. Three hundred points or more raise the odds to about 80 percent, according to the Holmes-Rahe model.

There's also a scale with questions for "non-adults," who I usually call children and teens. Both scales are below so you and your kid can evaluate yourselves.

FOR ADULTS

Life Event

1. Death of spouse 100
2. Divorce 73
3. Marital separation from mate 65
4. Detention in jail or other institution 63
5. Death of a close family member 63
6. Major personal injury or illness 53
7. Marriage 50
8. Being fired at work 47
9. Marital reconciliation with mate 45
10. Retirement from work 45
11. Major change in the health or behavior of a family member 44
12. Pregnancy 40

13. Sexual difficulties 39
14. Gaining a new family member (e.g., birth, adoption, older adult moving in, etc.) 39
15. Major business adjustment 39
16. Major change in financial state (i.e., a lot worse or better than usual) 38
17. Death of a close friend 37
18. Changing to a different line of work 36
19. Major change in number of arguments with spouse (i.e., a lot more or less) 35
20. Taking on a mortgage (for home, business, etc.) 31
21. Foreclosure on a mortgage or loan 30
22. Major change in responsibilities at work (e.g., promotion, demotion, etc.) 29
23. Son or daughter leaving home (marriage, college, military, etc.) 29
24. In-law troubles 29
25. Outstanding personal achievement 28
26. Spouse beginning or ceasing work outside the home 26
27. Beginning or ceasing formal schooling 26
28. Major change in living condition (e.g., new home, remodeling, deterioration, etc.) 25
29. Revision of personal habits (e.g., dress, associations, quit smoking, etc.) 24
30. Troubles with the boss 23
31. Major changes in working hours or conditions 20
32. Change in residence 20
33. Changing to a new school 20
34. Major change in usual type and/or amount of recreation 19
35. Major change in church activity (i.e., a lot more or less) 19

36. Major change in social activities (e.g., clubs, movies, visiting, etc.) 18
37. Taking on a small loan (e.g., car, home improvement, furniture, appliances, etc.) 17
38. Major change in sleeping habits (i.e., a lot more or less) 16
39. Major change in number of family get-togethers (i.e., a lot more or less) 15
40. Major change in eating habits (i.e., a lot more or less, eating hours, surroundings, etc.) 15
41. Vacation 13
42. Major holidays 12
43. Minor violations of the law (e.g., traffic tickets, jaywalking, etc.) 11

FOR "NON-ADULTS"

Life Event

1. Getting married 101
2. Death of parent 100
3. Unwed pregnancy 92
4. Acquiring a visible deformity 81
5. Divorce of parents 90
6. Fathering an unwed pregnancy 77
7. Becoming involved with drugs or alcohol 76
8. Jail sentence of parent for over one year 70
9. Marital separation of parents 69
10. Death of a brother or sister 68
11. Change in acceptance by peers 67
12. Pregnancy of unwed sister 64

13. Discovery of being an adopted child 63
14. Marriage of parent to stepparent 63
15. Death of a close friend 63
16. Having a visible congenital deformity 62
17. Going to a new school 59
18. Serious illness requiring hospitalization 58
19. Failure of a grade in school 56
20. Not making an extracurricular activity 55
21. Hospitalization of a parent 55
22. Jail sentence of parent for more than thirty days 53
23. Breaking up with boyfriend or girlfriend 53
24. Beginning to date 51
25. Suspension from school 50
26. Birth of a brother or sister 50
27. Increase in arguments between parents 47
28. Loss of job by parent 46
29. Outstanding personal achievement 46
30. Change in parent's financial status 45
31. Accepted at college of choice 43
32. Being a senior in high school 42
33. Hospitalization of a sibling 41
34. Increased absence of parent from home 38
35. Brother or sister leaving home 37
36. Death of grandparent 36
37. Addition of third adult to family 34
38. Starting a job 34
39. Marriage of brother or sister 26
40. Mother or father beginning work 26
41. Change in sleeping habits 16
42. Change in eating habits 15

Further Reading

GROUCHO MARX SAID THAT "OUTSIDE OF A DOG, A book is man's best friend. Inside of a dog, it's too dark to read." The following books sit on my shelf, are next to me in bed, under the pillow, piled in corners, full of dog-eared pages. They are the books I refer to the most, gift the most, and revere the most.

Donald Roberston is a professor, cognitive behavioral therapist, and good friend. He is a one-man conga line of Stoic wisdom. His best-selling books *How to Think Like a Roman Emperor: The Stoic Philosophy of Marcus Aurelius* and *Stoicism and the Art of Happiness: Practical Wisdom for Everyday Life* are great reads and wonderful introductions for anyone curious about Stoicism. Massimo Pigliucci is a professor of philosophy at the City College of New York and the author of *How to Be a Stoic: Using Ancient Philosophy to Live a Modern Life* and *A Field Guide to a Happy Life: 53 Brief Lessons for Living*. I first encountered him when I attended his lecture at the Ethical Culture Society and was inspired by his passion for teaching philosophy to life's students. I am indebted to Ryan Holiday for his efforts to bring

Stoicism to a modern audience. His books *The Daily Stoic: 366 Meditations on Wisdom, Perseverance, and the Art of Living* (with Stephen Hanselman) and *The Obstacle Is the Way: The Timeless Art of Turning Trials into Triumphs* are well-deserved best sellers. Ryan's Daily Stoic newsletter is a welcome arrival in my inbox; you can subscribe at ryanholiday.net. Reading Sharon Lebell's translation of Epictetus's *Enchiridion*, entitled *The Art of Living: The Classic Manual on Virtue, Happiness, and Effectiveness*, was a powerful experience for me and ignited the journey that led to this book. I recommend her speech titled "Women Don't Need Stoicism, Stoicism Needs Women," archived at modernstoics .com.

Among the classical writers, Aristotle's *The Nicomachean Ethics*, a series of letters to his son, influenced me both with his ideas and with his epistolary form. Seneca's *Letters from a Stoic* did the same. Marcus Aurelius's *Meditations* was the first book of Stoicism I read, twenty-five years ago. It lit the fuse for my philosophical pyrotechnics. Of course, the classical work closest to my soul is Epictetus's *Enchiridion*, which I own in multiple translations. I keep repurchasing this book; I wear out my copies because I live with them and love them so vigorously.

Viktor Frankl was a neurologist, psychiatrist, philosopher, survivor of the Holocaust, and author of the classic *Man's Search for Meaning*. In the extermination camps of Nazi Germany, Frankl came to a fundamental understanding of life that the Stoics would have recognized: "When we are no longer able to change a situation, we are challenged to change ourselves." Communist regimes were the basis for Witold Szarlowski's *Dancing Bears: True Stories of People Nostalgic for Life Under Tyranny*. *Thoughts of a Philosophical Fighter Pilot* by Admiral James B. Stockdale details how Stoicism helped him survive a brutal

POW camp in Vietnam. In his life and words, Admiral Stockdale leads us to understand that we can rise with dignity and prevail in adversity.

As someone with limited mobility, I am always galvanized by people who embody Epictetus's maxim, "It is a wise man who does not grieve for the things which he has not, but rejoices for those which he has." Sonia Purnell's *A Woman of No Importance* is the rip-roaring story of the one-legged socialite and spy Virginia Hall, whose wooden leg, named Cuthbert, was no impediment to heroism. My personal hero Bill Walton's book *Back from the Dead* is an exuberant memoir of his love and appreciation for life and the people and dogs and music and bicycles that helped him overcome grievous pain.

The philosopher and patron of libraries Francis Bacon wrote, "Some books are to be tasted, others to be swallowed and some few to be chewed and digested." These books have all taught me that obstacles are in our path not to stop us, but to inspire our strength, courage, and tenacity. They are a rich dietary source of wisdom and sustain me every time I crack their spines.

Acknowledgments

HERE WE ARE AT THE ACKNOWLEDGMENTS, KNOWN in publishing as "the back matter." This is the space where authors fawn and grovel and thank every well-known writer who crossed their path and mention how they hold a profound spot of affection for the writer's colony where they hatched their book. This is a transparent flex, just so the author can say they went to one. We all see through this self-promotion.

Thanking people at the end of a book is like putting together a guest list. Who will sit next to the man who was voted the "Sexiest Man Alive" twice? Who will sit at the cousins' table?

Writing is solitary; it's reading a million books, walking around and thinking about them, and then sitting down every day for two years to manipulate the twenty-six measly letters in our English alphabet to create a seventy-thousand-word love letter to life. If I actually spent time with all the great friends and esteemed colleagues who support me, I'd never get anything done.

This is my fourth book, and every one has been animated with the spirits of John and Jack Lambros and my beloved Dr.

Frank Petito. My friends, if you are looking for your names back here, you will have to read the book to see where I thank you.

I could go on and on, throwing roses at Andrew Muscato, Bill Murray, Lori Campbell, Lynn Fischer, Kate Firriolo, Greg Shano, Peg Donegan, Lizzie Bracco, Chris Vaccari, Jim Duffy, David Vigliano, Radzi, Debi Mazar, Aida, Ed Conlon, George and Amal Clooney, and Angel. I could give a shout out to Emi Ikkanda for believing in this book from the start. I would tip my hat and give a *mats-muts* to Christos Konstantakopolous for inviting me to think, be inspired, and crack the format of this book at the Oxbelly Lab. But modesty and lack of space prevent me from spitting out a list of names you, the reader, don't know.

Francis Gasparini is the only person I *will* name here, which for a chronic name dropper, underscores his importance in creating this book. Thank you, Francis, for being my writing partner and collaborator for the past two decades.

Francis's Acknowledgments: Thank you to my wife, Jennifer Wise, for inspiring me and laughing at me. Thank you to my daughter, Maria Lucia Gasparini, for her drawing of Cuthbert and for her active excitement and interest when I shared stories from the manuscript over dinner about Virginia Hall, the Monkey Busters, and the dancing bears of Bulgaria. Thank you to my parents, Frank and Lucille Gasparini, for raising me in a home stocked with books. My extra special thanks to Pat Wise, who had to listen to me typing and cackling for hours on end every day for months.

John Eder is a photographer and illustrator who created the images that adorn this book. To see more of his work, check out JohnEder.com

ONDREA BARBE

Karen Duffy is the *New York Times* best-selling author of *Model Patient*. She is a producer, actress, and former MTV VJ. She has written for the *New York Times*, the *Wall Street Journal*, and O, *The Oprah Magazine*. She lives in New York.